Samuel A. McPhetres

A Political Manual for the Campaign of 1868

Samuel A. McPhetres

A Political Manual for the Campaign of 1868

ISBN/EAN: 9783337425722

Printed in Europe, USA, Canada, Australia, Japan

Cover: Foto ©ninafisch / pixelio.de

More available books at **www.hansebooks.com**

A

POLITICAL MANUAL

FOR THE

CAMPAIGN OF 1868,

FOR USE IN THE

NEW ENGLAND STATES,

CONTAINING THE POPULATION AND LATEST ELECTION
RETURNS OF EVERY TOWN IN NEW ENGLAND,
AND OF EVERY STATE IN THE UNION,
PARTY PLATFORMS, AND OTHER
VALUABLE INFORMATION.

By S. A. McPhetres.

BOSTON:

A. WILLIAMS AND COMPANY,

100 WASHINGTON STREET.

1868.

Press of Stone & Huse, ... Lowell, Mass.

TABLE OF CONTENTS.

Entered according to Act of Congress in the year 1868 by S. A. McPHETRES in the Clerk's office of the District Court of Massachusetts.

INTRODUCTORY.

Preceding almost every important election in New England recently, the author has heard frequent inquiries for some paper or book which gave the returns by towns at the last previous election. In New England we feel proud of our town system, and the election returns are made by towns; in nearly every other State no political division below counties is regarded as of any great importance. The "Tribune" and "Democratic" almanacs give tables of returns by counties in nearly every State, which answers the demand for reference outside of New England. About the time of the New Hampshire election, last March, the compiler first thought of publishing the work now presented, for use in the Presidential Campaign of 1868. Official figures have been obtained from the office of each Secretary of State, at considerable trouble and expense, and the tables of votes are believed to be in all cases reliable.

The census of each town for 1850 and 1860 are also given, and those taken under authority of the States of Massachusetts and Rhode Island in 1865. It is believed that this feature will greatly add to the value of the work, and cause it to be preserved for reference after the next election returns shall have given place to later ones. The arrangement of towns alphabetically has involved great labor, but it is believed will render the work more acceptable to those who often desire to refer to some town with whose geographical location they may not be altogether familiar. The names of 1494 cities, towns and voting-places are given, divided as follows : Maine, 485; New Hampshire, 231 : Vermont, 245; Massachusetts, 336; Rhode Island, 34; Connecticut, 163. In one or two States there is a discrepancy between the votes of some towns and counties, and the total official vote. In these cases errors of omission, or mistakes were made by town officers in the names of candidates, and the votes were credited to "scattering," or omitted altogether. The compiler has given such votes as they should have been returned.

In addition to the census and election returns of New England towns, other, and by no means secondary, features of the "Manual," it is trusted, will prove convenient and useful : such as the popular vote of all the States taking part in the elections for President in 1860 and 1864; popular vote at most recent elections; times of elections; area of each State and population in 1850 and 1860, with the classes at the latter period; Governors of States; United States Government, with the majority for each Representative in Congress at his last election; History of Impeachment; summary of the proceedings of the Republican and Democratic National Conventions, the platform adopted by each, sketches of the candidates, with the sentiments of each as presented in his letter of acceptance, &c.

It has been the purpose of the author to make this "Manual" acceptable as a work of reference, alike to Democrats, Conservatives, Republicans and Radicals, by omitting everything that might give it a partizan character; and it is sent forth with the hope that it may to some extent benefit every one into whose hands it may chance to fall.

Lowell, July, 1868.

NEW ENGLAND.

Though relatively only a small section of the great American Union, New England has a larger territory than the kingdom of Portugal, is two-thirds as large as Italy, one-third as large as Spain, and half as large as England and Ireland combined. Maine exceeds in territorial extent Bavaria with its four and one-half millions of people, is twice as large as Switzerland with its two and one-half millions of inhabitants, and more than twice as large as Holland with its three and one-half millions of Dutchmen, and is nearly three times as large as Hanover. Saxony, with less than two-thirds the territorial extent of New Hampshire, has six times as large a population. Vermont and Rhode Island united are equal in extent to Belgium, with its four and one half millions of souls; and Wurtemburg, with less territory than Massachusetts, has half a million more people. The State of Connecticut is larger than the Roman States, the dominion of Pius Ninth.

Constant, powerful and well rewarded efforts have been made and are still making, through the medium of the press, by lecturers, emigrant aid societies, agents and circulars to convince New England people that happiness, prosperity and wealth are sure anywhere and everywhere save in the East. Nor have our own officials and citizens always endeavored to combat these ideas and efforts; for it is only a few years since that a patriotic, and now lamented, Governor of a New England State, in his annual message to the Legislature, recommended the adoption of some measure to aid young women to leave the State and seek homes elsewhere.

These arguments and efforts have had their influence not only to induce natives of New England to immigrate, and to a great extent decrease the population in certain localities, as the tables published elsewhere prove, but to turn to some extent the tide which might have increased her population by inducing industrious and thrifty outsiders to settle within her borders. Hundreds of thousands of the young, tens of thousands of

the middle-aged, and thousands of those past the me-
ridian of life, have bid farewell to the homes, associa-
tions and scenes of New England, and sought new ones
in distant States and Territories.   In 1850 the number
of persons of New England birth in the United States
was 2,821,823, of whom 453,896 resided outside of the
six New England States.   In 1860 the number of natives
of New England had increased to 3,144,598, of whom
560,336 — or more than one-sixth — resided elsewhere.
The natural increase of natives was, therefore, 322,775,
while the immigrants had increased 106,440, showing
that the immigration equalled one-third of those born.
Taking the estimate for deaths it is safe to say that the
number of those leaving New England between the two
decennial periods must have been 15,000 or 16,000 annu-
ally.   The New Englanders resident in New York in 1860
amounted to 177,981, more than the population of Rhode
Island that year.   Illinois had received 66,093; Wisconsin, 54,340; Ohio, 53,386; Michigan, 38,106; California,
32,269; Pennsylvania, 25,555; Iowa, 25,040; Minnesota,
18,822; Indiana, 12,307, and other States and Territories
smaller numbers.   The New England population of eight
of those called the Western States, increased 100,000 in
ten years.   Some of these immigrants no doubt im-
proved their condition, but tens of thousands were no
better off than when they left their former homes in
New England, but want of means or pride have pre-
vented them from returning.

Statistics prove the fact that New England, if older,
and by many represented as worn out, gives better returns even for agricultural labor, than some of the
newer States.   The *Virginia Advertiser*, published at
Lynchburg, in that State, a few months ago, gave some
comparisons, which coming from an impartial source is
worthy of place here.   Under the head of " Some Facts
worth Knowing " the *Advertiser* says :

We have taken the trouble to compile from the Report of the
Commissioner of Agriculture, for 1865, the following interesting
table, exhibiting at a glance the relative productiveness and value
of crops of the New England States and six of the Western States,
viz: Ohio, Indiana, Illinois, Missouri, Iowa and Minnesota.   We
have selected the six New England States as being considered the

least productive agricultural States of any on the Atlantic slope, and the six named Western States as being among the most productive agricultural States of the West, and these we propose to compare by the light of the official statistics furnished by the Department of Agriculture for four years, from 1862 to 1865 inclusive. We have selected all of the staple crops of the two sections, and believe the table presents as fair a comparison as can be made between them.

	Average yield per year.		Aver. value pr. acre.	
	N. Eng.	W. States.	N. Eng.	W. States.
Corn, bushels,	33½	33¾	$ 43.31	$ 22.09
Wheat, "	15¼	14	30.29	15.28
Oats, "	31	28½	20.59	12.36
Potatoes, "	124¾	100⅓	74.75	59.66
Hay, pounds,	2182	3129	18.94	16.25
Tobacco, "	1031½	856½	236.50	120.16

We confess that when we began to make this examination we were not entirely prepared for the result obtained. Knowing as we did, the superiority of the East over the West, still we had not thought that BARREN NEW ENGLAND was ahead even in the QUANTITY produced. It will be observed by examining the above table that while the Eastern States are a little ahead in quantity produced, the VALUE PER ACRE ARE NEARLY DOUBLE those of the West. In other words a farmer in New England will make nearly twice as much money from the cultivation of one acre of land as the farmer in the Western States. Though this result is contrary to the commonly received opinion we believe it to be correct.

The Virginia editor proceeds to show that his section is far behind the West, and consequently greatly behind New England. It is far from the purpose of the writer to say anything against the great—the patriotic West—against Illinois, which has given us a Lincoln and a Grant; against Ohio, the home of a Sherman, a Sheridan and a Brough; against Indiana, the residence of a Wallace, a Morton and a Colfax, or against other States which have given the country so any eminent men, wise in council, and so many patriotic men, brave in war. All honor to the West; may it prosper and increase in wealth and power. But it is believed the West does not need the young life-blood of New England to ensure her prosperity, which while they " enrich her makes us poor indeed." The outpouring tide of immigrants should not be checked by detracting from the West, and fermenting feelings of envy and distrust which never result in good, but by inspiring the East with new zeal, and making it for the interest of the young to remain on the soil on which they were born.

THE SOUTHERN ELECTORAL COLLEGE BILL.

The following is a copy of the bill excluding certain States from voting for President, vetoed by the President, but passed by Congress over the veto, July 20th, 1868.

That none of the States whose inhabitants were lately in rebellion, and which States are not now represented in Congress, shall be entitled to representation in the electoral college for the choice of President and Vice President of the United States, nor shall any electoral votes be received or counted from any of such States, unless at the time prescribed by law for the choice of electors the people of such States, pursuant to acts of Congress in that behalf, shall have since the 4th of March, 1867, adopted a constitution of State government under which a State government shall have been organized and shall be in operation, and unless such election of electors shall have been made under the authority of such constitution and government, and such States shall have also become entitled to representation in Congress, pursuant to acts of Congress in that behalf.

ADDITIONAL RETURNS, ERRATA, ETC.

ALABAMA.—J. B. Callis has been qualified as Representative in Congress from the 5th District, instead of Joseph W. Burke, who was first reported elected, and whose name is given on page 62. George E. Spencer has been elected United States Senator for the term ending in 1873, and Willard Warner, for the term ending in 1871.

INDIANA.—George W. Julian, Representative in Congress, has been nominated for re-election.

MISSISSIPPI.—The vote on the Constitution is reported as follows: Yeas, 56,231; Nays, 63,860; majority for rejection, 7,629. The Democratic State ticket is elected. The members of Congress are: District 1, Charles H. Townsend; 2, T. N. Martin; 3, G. P. M. Turner; 4, George C. McKee; 5, William T. Martin. Mr. McKee is a Republican; the others Democrats.

OHIO.—The Republican vote in 1867, on page 57, should read 243,605 instead of 263,605. The majority given—2,983 Republican—is correct.

OREGON.—Vote for Congressmen, 1868: Joseph S. Smith, Democrat, 11,789; David Logan, Republican, 10,580. Democratic majority, 1,209.

VERMONT.—The vote for Governor commencing on page 34 is that of 1867, not 1868.

PRESIDENTIAL ELECTORAL VOTE SINCE 1788.

The following shows the votes for President and Vice President since the establishment of our National Government. Previous to 1804, the electors voted for two persons, but did not designate which should be President and which Vice President. A majority of electoral votes, as now, were required to elect the President, but the person receiving the second highest number of votes became Vice President. At the first two elections there were no party divisions.

1788. George Washington, 69; John Adams, 34; John Jay, 9; R. H. Harrison, 6; John Rutledge, 6; John Hancock, 4; George Clinton, 3; Samuel Huntington, 2; John Milton, 2; John Armstrong, 1; Edward Telfair, 1; Benjamin Lincoln, 1.

1792. George Washington, 132; John Adams, 77; George Clinton, 50; Thomas Jefferson, 4; Aaron Burr, 1.

1796. John Adams, Federalist, 71; Thomas Jefferson Republican, 68; Thomas Pinckney, Fed., 59; Samuel Adams, Rep., 15; Oliver Ellsworth, Fed., 11; George Clinton, 7; John Jay, 5; James Iredell, 3; George Washington, 2; Samuel Johnston, 2; John Henry, 2; Charles C. Pinckney, 1.
[Mr. Jefferson was the Republican candidate for President, but receiving the second highest number of votes, became Vice President.]

1800. Thomas Jefferson, Republican, 73; Aaron Burr, Rep., 73; John Adams, Federalist, 65; Charles C. Pinckney, Fed., 64; John Jay, Fed., 1.
[Mr. Burr was the Republican candidate for Vice President, but there being a tie, the House of Representatives after a protracted contest elected Mr. Jefferson President by the votes of ten States; to four for Mr. Burr and 2 blanks. The Federalists preferred the latter "as a choice of two evils," as they then thought. The Constitution was amended so that the electors should thereafter vote separately for President and Vice President.]

1804. *President:* Thomas Jefferson, Republican, 162; Charles C. Pinckney, Federalist, 14. *Vice President:* George Clinton, Rep., 162; Rufus King, Fed., 14.

1808. *President:* James Madison, Republican, 122; Charles C. Pinckney, Federalist, 47; George Clinton, Rep., 6. *Vice President:* George Clinton, Rep., 113; Rufus King, Fed., 47; John Langdon, Rep., 9; James Madison, Rep., 3; James Monroe, Rep., 3.

1812. *President:* James Madison, Republican, 128; De Witt Clinton, Anti-War, 89. *Vice President:* Elbridge Gerry, Rep., 131; Jared Ingersoll, Anti-War, 86.

1816. *President:* James Monroe, Republican, 183; Rufus King, Federalist, 34. *Vice President:* Daniel D. Tompkins, Rep., 183; John E. Howard, Fed., 22; James Ross, Fed., 5; John Marshall, Fed., 4; Robert G. Harper, Fed., 3.

1820. *President:* James Monroe, 228; John Quincy Adams, 1. *Vice President:* Daniel D. Tompkins, 215; Richard Stockton, 8; Daniel Rodney, 4; Robert G. Harper, 1; Richard Rush, 1.

1824. *President:* Andrew Jackson, Democrat, 99; John Quincy Adams, Republican, 84; William H. Crawford, Caucus, 41; Henry Clay, Rep., 37. *Vice President:* John C. Calhoun, Dem. and Rep., 182; Nathan Sanford, Rep., 30; Nathaniel Macon, Dem., 24; Andrew Jackson, Dem., 13, Martin Van Buren, Dem., 9; Henry Clay, Rep., 2. Popular vote for President: Jackson, 155,872; Adams, 105,321; Crawford, 44,282; Clay, 46,587.

[There having been no choice by the electors for President in 1824, the House of Representatives made choice of John Quincy Adams, giving him the votes of 13 States, to 7 for Andrew Jackson, and 4 for William H. Crawford.]

1828. *President:* Andrew Jackson, Democrat, 178; John Quincy Adams, National Republican, 83. *Vice President:* John C. Calhoun, Dem., 171; Richard Rush, Nat. Rep., 83; William Smith, Dem., 7. Popular vote for President: Jackson, 647,231; Adams, 509,097.

1832. *President:* Andrew Jackson, Democrat, 219; Henry Clay, Whig, 49; John Floyd, Nullifier, 11; William Wirt, Anti-Mason, 7. *Vice President:* Martin Van Buren, Dem., 189; John Sergeant, Whig, 49; William Wilkins, Dem., 30; Henry Lee, Null., 11; Amos Ellmaker, Anti-Mason, 7. Popular vote for President: Jackson, 687,502; Clay and others, 530,189.

1836. *President:* Martin Van Buren, Democrat, 170; William H. Harrison, Whig, 73; Hugh L. White, Whig, 26; Daniel Webster, Whig, 14; Willie P. Mangum, Whig, 11. *Vice President:* Richard M. Johnson, Dem., 147; Francis Granger, Whig, 77; John Tyler, Whig, 47; William Smith, Dem., 23. Popular vote for President: Van Buren, 761,549; Harrison and others, 736,656.

[The other candidates having tied Mr. Johnson for Vice President in the electoral colleges, the latter was elected by the Senate over Mr. Granger.]

1840. *President:* William H. Harrison, Whig, 234; Martin Van Buren, Democrat, 60. *Vice President:* John Tyler, Whig, 234; Richard M. Johnson, Dem., 48; Littleton W. Tazewell, Dem., 11; James K. Polk, Dem., 1. Popular vote for President: Harrison, 1,275,011; Van Buren, 1,122,912; Birney, Liberty, 7,059.

1844. *President:* James K. Polk, Dem., 170; Henry Clay, Whig, 105. *Vice President:* George M. Dallas, Dem., 170; Theodore Frelinghuysen, Whig, 105. Popular vote for President: Polk, 1,337,243; Clay, 1,299,062; Birney, Liberty, 62,300.

1848. *President:* Zachary Taylor, Whig, 163; Lewis Cass, Democrat, 127. *Vice President:* Millard Fillmore, Whig, 163; William O. Butler, Dem., 127. Popular vote for President: Taylor, 1,360,099; Cass, 1,220,544; Van Buren, Free Soil, 291,263.

1852. *President*: Franklin Pierce, Democrat, 254; Winfield Scott, Whig, 42. *Vice President*: William R. King, Dem., 254; William A. Graham, Whig, 42. Popular vote for President: Pierce, 1,601,274; Scott, 1,386,580; Hale, Free Soil, 155,825.

1856. *President*: James Buchanan, Dem., 174; John C. Fremont, Republican, 114; Millard Fillmore, American, 8. *Vice President*: John C. Breckinridge, Dem., 174; William L. Dayton, Rep., 114; Andrew J. Donelson, American, 8. Popular vote for President: Buchanan, 1,838,229; Fremont, 1,342,164; Fillmore, 874,625.

[For the electoral and popular votes for President and Vice President in 1860 and 1864 see page 56 of this Manual.]

ALASKA. This territory for which Congress, just before its adjournment, appropriated $7,200,000, the price agreed upon to be paid Russia, contains a territory estimated at from 400,000 to 570,000 square miles, thus adding to upward of 3,000,000 square miles in the United States previously, that large amount of territory. The coast is said to extend over 4,000 miles, and the fisheries and furs are very valuable, but whether in other respects it will be largely profitable is yet to be determined. Its population, owing to the climate, is small, being estimated from 40,000 to 75,000.

AMNESTY. The amnesty proclamation of President Johnson, issued July 4th, 1868, pardons every person who, directly or indirectly, participated in the late insurrection or rebellion, excepting such persons as may be under presentment or indictment in any Court of the United States upon a charge of treason or other felony, with restoration of all rights of property except as to slaves, and except also as to any property of which any person may have been legally divested under the laws of the United States.

EQUAL and exact justice to all men, of whatever state or persuasion, religious or political. . . . . Economy in the public expense, that labor may be lightly burdened; the honest payment of our debts, and sacred preservation of the public faith.— THOMAS JEFFERSON'S *first inaugural address*.

THE PUBLIC DEBT. The public debt of the United States at its highest point, 31st of August, 1865, was $2,757,689,571 over the amount of cash in the Treasury. On the 1st of June, 1868, it was $2,510,245,886.

MEMBERS OF NATIONAL COMMITTEES.

Republican.	Democratic.
Ala.—Jas. P. Stow, Montgomery,	John Forsyth, Mobile,
Ark.—B. F. Rice, Little Rock,	J. M. Harrell, Little Rock,
Cal.—G. C. Gorham, San Francisco,	John Bigler, San Francisco,
Ct.—H. H. Starkweather, Norwich,	Wm. M. Converse, Franklin
Del.—E. G. Bradford, Wilmington,	Sam'l Townsend, Newcastle,
Fla.—S. B. Conover, Lake City,	C. E. Dyke, Tallahassee,
Ga.—J. H. Caldwell, Lagrange,	A. H. Colquitt, Albany,
Ill.—J. R. Jones, Chicago,	W. F. Story, Chicago,
Ind.—C. M. Allen, Vincennes,	W. E. Niblack, Vincennes,
Iowa—Josiah Tracy, Burlington,	D. O. Finch, DesMoines,
Kan.—J. A. Martin, Atchison,	I. E. Eaton, Leavenworth,
Ken.—A. A. Burton, Lancaster,	T. C. McCreery, Owensboro',
La.—M. H. Southworth, N. Orleans,	Jas. McCloskey, New Orleans,
Me.—Lewis Barker, Stetson,	S. R. Lyman, Portland,
Md.—C. C. Fulton, Baltimore,	Odin Bowie, Pr. George,
Mass.—Wm. Claflin, Boston,	F. O. Prince, Boston,
Mich.—M. Giddings, Kalamazoo,	W. A. Moore, Detroit,
Minn.—J. T. Averill, St. Paul,	Charles W. Nash, St. Paul,
Miss.—A. C. Fisk, Vicksburg,	Charles E. Hooker, Jackson,
Mo.—B. F. Loan, St. Joseph,	Charles A. Zwarts, St. Louis,
Neb.—E. B. Taylor, Omaha,	G. L. Miller, Omaha,
Nev.—C. E. DeLong, Va. City,	J. W. McCorkle, Va. City,
N. H.—W. E. Chandler, Wash., D. C.,	Harry Bingham, Littleton,
N. J.—James Gopsill, Jersey City,	John McGregor, Newark,
N. Y.—Horace Greeley, New York,	August Belmont, New York,
N. C.—William Sloan, Charlotte,	Thomas Bragg, Raleigh,
Ohio—B. R. Cowen, Bellaire,	J. G. Thompson, Columbus,
Ore.—H. W. Corbett, Portland,	J. C. Hawthorn, Portland,
Pa.—William H. Kemble, Phila.,	Isaac Eskister, Lancaster,
R. I.—L. B. Frieze, Providence,	Gid. Bradford, Charlestown,
S. C.—J. H. Jenks, Charleston,	C. H. Simonton, Charleston,
Tenn.—W. B. Stokes, Liberty,	J. W. Leftwick, Memphis,
Tex.—A. J. Hamilton, Austin,	John Hancock, Austin,
Vt.—T. W. Park, No. Bennington,	H. B. Smith, Milton,
Va.—Franklin Stearns, Richmond,	John Goode, Norfolk,
W. Va.—S. D. Karns, Parkersburg,	John Hall, Port Pleasant,
Wis.—David Atwood, Madison,	F. W. Horn, Cedartown,

Wm. Claflin, Boston, Mass., *Chm.*, August Belmont, N. Y., *Chm.*,
W. E. Chandler, Wash'n, D. C. *Sec.* F. O. Prince, Boston, *Sec.*

POPULATION AND VOTE OF MAINE.

Population in 1850 and 1860 by each United States census. Candidates for Governor in 1867: Joshua L. Chamberlain, Republican; Eben F. Pillsbury, Democrat. The vote for Governor marked *u* is unofficial.

Town.	County.	Population 1850	1860	Governor '67. Chamb.	Pills.
Abbott,	Piscataquis,	747	796	102	35
Acton,	York,	1359	1218	146	114
Addison,	Washington,	1152	1272	64	92
Albany,	Oxford,	747	813	69	65
Albion,	Kennebec,	1604	1554	159	144
Albion Gore,	"	110			
Alexander,	Washington,	544	445	32	38
Alfred,	York,	1319	1256	172	133
Alna,	Lincoln,	916	805	112	76
Alva,	Aroostook,			28	2
Alton,	Penobscot,	252	531	36	46
Amherst,	Hancock,	323	384	32	38
Amity,	Aroostook,	256	302	21	28
Andover,	Oxford,	710	814	99	56
Anson,	Somerset,	2016	2001	168	194
Appleton,	Knox,	1727	1573	142	183
Argyle,	Penobscot,	338	379	37	40
Arrowsic,	Sagadahoc,	311	347	20	29
Ashland,	Aroostook,		606	40	17
Athens,	Somerset,	1460	1417	157	135
Atkinson,	Piscataquis,	895	897	81	58
Auburn,	Androscoggin,	2840	4022	711	386
Augusta,	Kennebec,	8225	*7609	834	759
Aurora,	Hancock,	217	277	14	25
Avon,	Franklin,	778	802	75	63
Baileyville,	Washington,	431	363	13	30
Baldwin,	Cumberland,	1100	1227	131	123
Bancroft,	Aroostook,	157	304	15	22
Bangor,	Penobscot,	14432	16407	1305	1054
Baring,	Washington,	380	409	26	7
Barnard,	Piscataquis,	181	172	4	15
Bath,	Sagadahoc,	8020	8076	761	386
Beddington,	Washington,	147	144	8	7
Belfast,	Waldo,	5051	5520	451	327
Belfast plantation,	Aroostook,	259	287		
Belgrade,	Kennebec,	1722	1592	140	173
Belmont,	Waldo,	1486	†686	40	89
Benedicta,	Aroostook,	325	307		*u*45
Benton,	Kennebec,	1189	1183	122	156
Berwick,	York,	2121	2155	239	242
Bethel,	Oxford,	2253	2523	229	124

* Part of Manchester set off.   † Morrill set off.

Town.	County.	1850	1860	Chamb.	Pills.
Biddeford,	York,	6095	9349	605	834
Bingham,	Somerset,	752	831	62	80
Blanchard,	Piscataquis,	192	164	24	11
Bloomfield,	Somerset,	1301	1397 To Skowhegan
Bluehill,	Hancock,	1939	1993	131	91
Boothbay,	Lincoln,	2504	2857	185	118
Bowdoin,	Sagadahoc,	1857	1744	128 .	76
Bowdoinham,	"	2382	2343	230 •	79
Bowerbank,	Piscataquis,	173	101	7	9
Bradford,	Penobscot,	1296	1558	171	91
Bradley,	"	796	844	72	37
Bremen,	Lincoln,	891	907	65	48
Brewer,	Penobscot,	2628	2835	277	92
Bridgewater,	Aroostook,	143	491	21	20
Bridgton,	Cumberland,	2710	2556	347	228
Brighton,	Somerset,	748	733	32	75
Bristol,	Lincoln,	2931	3335	227	261
Brooklyn,	Hancock,	1002	1043	108	45
Brooks,	Waldo,	1021	988	129	43
Brooksville,	Hancock,	1333	1428	73	85
Brownfield,	Oxford,	1320	1398	150	111
Brownville,	Piscataquis,	787	793	99	22
Brunswick,	Cumberland,	4977	4723	416	395
Buckfield,	Oxford,	1657	1705	198	203
Bucksport,	Hancock,	3381	3554	300	171
Burlington,	Penobscot,	481	578	33	51
Burnham,	Waldo,	784	857	58	97
Buxton, .	York,	2095	2853	315	308
Byron,	Oxford,	296	323	u25	11
Calais,	Washington,	4749	5621	436	93
Cambridge,	Somerset,	487	516	43	71
Camden,	Knox,	4005	4588	417	384
Canaan,	Somerset,	1696	1715	139	213
Canton,	Oxford,	926	1025	124	125
Cape Elizabeth,	Cumberland,	2082	3278	316	312
Carmel,	Penobscot,	1225	1271	131	159
Carratunk,	Somerset,		227	29	19
Carroll,	Penobscot,	401	470	33	49
Carthage,	Franklin,	420	503	42	43
Casco,	Cumberland,	1046	1116	106	109
Castine,	Hancock,	1260	1357	119	70
Castle Hill,	Aroostook,			15	5
Centerville,	Washington,	178	191	5	32
Charleston,	Penobscot,	1283	1430	130	168
Charlotte,	Washington,	718	611	40	32
Chelsea,	Kennebec,	New	1024	63	55
Cherryfield,	Washington,	1648	1755	212	79
Chester,	Penobscot,	340	318	36	9
Chesterville,	Franklin,	1142	1110	142	79
China,	Kennebec,	2769	2719	270	185
Clifton,	Penobscot,	306	307	39	23
Clinton,	Kennebec,	1743	1803	186	194
Clinton Gore,	"	195	219	21	23

Town.	County.	1850	1860	Chamb.	Pills.
Codyville plan.,	Washington,			5	12
Columbia,	"	1140	1265	50	73
Columbia Falls,	"	New town,		42	63
Concord,	Somerset,	550	540	32	50
Cooper,	Washington,	562	468	20	33
Corinna,	Penobscot,	1550	1597	172	97
Corinth,	"	1600	1730	189	142
Cornish,	York,	1144	1153	147	117
Cornville,	Somerset,	1260	1141	118	43
Cranberry Isles,	Hancock,	283	347	22	24
Crawford,	Washington,	324	273	10	21
Crystal plantation,	Aroostook,			31	10
Cumberland,	Cumberland,	1656	1713	115	139
Cushing,	Knox,	807	796	27	107
Cutler,	Washington,	820	890	20	110
Daigle plantation,	Aroostook,			45	
Dallas plantation,	Franklin,			9	22
Damariscotta,	Lincoln,	1328	1366	172	85
Danforth,	Washington,	168	283	17	13
Danville,	Androscoggin,	1636	1322	To Auburn.	
Dayton,	York,	New	701	74	97
Dayton plantation,	Aroostook,	49	49	26	4
Deblois,	Washington,		131	9	11
Dedham,	Hancock,	546	495	54	29
Deer Isle,	"	3037	3590	74	152
Denmark,	Oxford,	1203	1171	101	143
Dennysville,	Washington,	458	485	76	6
Detroit,	Somerset,	517	659	67	96
Dexter,	Penobscot,	1948	2363	228	163
Dion plantation,	Aroostook,			38	73
Dixfield,	Oxford,	1180	1181	99	156
Dixmont,	Penobscot,	1605	1442	188	52
Dover,	Piscataquis,	1927	1970	272	107
Dresden,	Lincoln,	1419	1247	102	119
Drew plantation,	Penobscot,			15	1
Durham,	Androscoggin,	1886	1623	167	157
Eastbrook,	Hancock,	212	221	18	18
East Livermore,	Androscoggin,	891	1029	113	35
East Machias,	Washington,	1905	2181	150	200
Easton,	Aroostook,			41	12
Eastport,	Washington,	4125	3850	275	151
Eaton plantation,	Aroostook,	188	320	23	55
Eddington,	Penobscot,	696	856	74	77
Eden,	Hancock,	1127	1247	83	72
Edgecomb,	Lincoln,	1231	1112	82	58
Edinburg,	Penobscot,	93	48	5	4
Edmunds,	Washington,	446	414	34	17
Elliot,	York,	1803	1767	187	183
Elliotsville,	Piscataquis,	102	59		
Ellsworth,	Hancock,	4009	4658	393	224
Embden,	Somerset,	971	1041	70	113
Enfield,	Penobscot,	396	526	50	32
Etna,	"	802	849	110	30

Town.	County.	1850	1860	Chamb.	Pills.
Eustis plantation,	Franklin,		301	21	45
Exeter,	Penobscot,	1853	1783	175	129
Fairfield,	Somerset,	2452	2753	351	212
Falmouth,	Cumberland,	2157	1935	175	171
Farmingdale,	Kennebec,	New	896	83	60
Farmington,	Franklin,	2725	3106	393	234
Fayette,	Kennebec,	1085	910	105	38
Flag Staff plan.,	Somerset,			12	6
Fort Fairfield,	Aroostook,	401	901	177	75
Fort Kent,	"			6	64
Forestville plan.,	"		179	*u*12	32
Forks,	Somerset,			10	5
Foxcroft,	Piscataquis,	1045	1102	176	47
Franklin,	Hancock,	736	1004	106	47
Franklin plan.,	Oxford,	188	335	4	22
Frankfort,	Waldo,	4233	*2143	48	165
Freedom,	"	948	849	45	131
Freeman,	Franklin,	762	666	59	93
Freeport,	Cumberland,	2629	2792	289	147
Fremont plan.,	Aroostook,			*u*12	32
Friendship,	Knox,	691	770	32	103
Fryeburg,	Oxford,	1523	1623	184	126
Gardiner,	Kennebec,	6486	†4487	499	279
Garland,	Penobscot,	1247	1498	181	102
Georgetown,	Sagadahoc,	1121	1254	49	100
Getchell plan.,	Franklin,		134		
Gilead,	Oxford,	359	347	34	20
Glenburn,	Penobscot,	905	741	58	62
Glenwood,	Aroostook,		36	17	11
Golden Ridge,	"	194			
Gouldsborough,	Hancock,	1400	1717	97	142
Gorham,	Cumberland,	3088	3252	321	229
Grafton,	Oxford,		111	10	19
Grant Isle,	Aroostook,		145		
Gray,	Cumberland,	1788	1767	168	213
Greenbush,	Penobscot,	457	656	37	50
Greene,	Androscoggin,	1348	1224	127	82
Greenfield,	Penobscot,	305	359	39	27
Greenville,	Piscataquis,	326	310	22	33
Greenwood,	Oxford,	1118	878	75	77
Guilford,	Piscataquis,	834	837	86	110
Hallowell,	Kennebec,	4769	‡2435	268	140
Hamlin's Grant,	Oxford,	108	79	9	5
Hamlin plantation,	Aroostook,			11	42
Hampden,	Penobscot,	3195	3085	302	199
Hancock,	Aroostook,	592			
Hancock,	Hancock,	960	923	89	41
Hanover,	Oxford,	266	257	27	23
Harmony,	Somerset,	1107	1081	131	49
Harpswell,	Cumberland,	1534	1603	127	138

* Winterport set off. † West Gardiner and Farmingdale set off.
‡ Chelsea and part of Manchester set off.

Town.	County.	1850	1860	Chamb.	Pills.
Harrington,	Washington,	963	1130	66	88
Harrison,	Cumberland,	1416	1251	135	116
Hartford,	Oxford,	1293	1156	126	108
Hartland,	Somerset,	960	1050	108	96
Haynesville,	Aroostook,	96	169	5	4
Hebron,	Oxford,	839	895	114	47
Hermon,	Penobscot,	1374	1433	139	99
Hiram,	Oxford,	1210	1283	164	137
Hodgdon,	Aroostook,	862	963	62	37
Holden,	Penobscot,	New	805	82	50
Hollis,	York,	2683	*1683	198	216
Hope,	Knox,	1108	1064	130	64
Houlton,	Aroostook,	1453	2035	199	110
Howland,	Penobscot,	214	174	27	9
Hudson,	"	717	771	34	89
Industry,	Franklin,	1041	827	78	64
Island Falls plan.,	Aroostook,			22	1
Islesborough,	Waldo,	984	1276	71	78
Jackson,	"	833	827	99	48
Jay,	Franklin,	1733	1680	175	149
Jefferson,	Lincoln,	2225	2121	217	166
Jonesborough,	Washington,	466	518	15	56
Jonesport,	"	826	1148	19	107
Katahdin,	Piscataquis,	158			
Kenduskeag,	Penobscot,	New	816	82	48
Kennebunk,	York,	2650	2679	259	243
Kennebunkport,	"	2706	2668	246	296
Kingfield,	Franklin,	662	670	55	75
Kingsbury,	Piscataquis,	181	191	16	17
Kittery,	York,	2706	2974	374	226
Knox,	Waldo,	1102	1074	100	119
Lagrange,	Penobscot,	482	690	68	24
Lang plantation,	Franklin,			4	5
Leavitt plantation	Aroostook,			3	9
Lebanon,	York,	2208	2040	262	120
Lee,	Penobscot,	917	939	69	108
Leeds,	Androscoggin,	1652	1390	158	110
Levant,	Penobscot,	1841	1301	136	73
Lewiston,	Androscoggin,	3584	7424	791	304
Lexington,	Somerset,	538	495	31	63
Liberty,	Waldo,	1116	1095	111	73
Limerick,	York,	1473	1441	161	161
Limestone plan.,	Aroostook,		161		
Limington,	York,	2116	2004	236	214
Lincoln,	Penobscot,	1356	1631	195	42
Lincoln plantation,	Oxford,		76	4	5
Lincolnville,	Waldo,	2174	2075	193	199
Linneus,	Aroostook,	561	785	85	64
Lisbon,	Androscoggin,	1495	1376	255	97
Litchfield,	Kennebec,	2100	1702	218	55
Littleton,	Aroostook,		543	74	15

* Dayton set off.

Town.	County.	1850	1860	Chamb:	Pills.
Livermore,	Androscoggin,	1764	1597	202	87
Long Island,	Hancock,	152	188		
Lovell,	Oxford,	1193	1339	142	124
Lowell,	Penobscot,	378	556	38	55
Ludlow,	Aroostook,			20	16
Lubec,	Washington,	2814	2555	128	86
Lyman,	York,	1376	1307	159	133
Lyndon,	Aroostook,	203	297	55	20
Machias,	Washington,	1590	2256	202	191
Machiasport,	"	1266	1502	34	108
Macwahoc plan.,	Aroostook,		202	u10	10
Madawaska,	"	1276	585	7	64
Madison,	Somerset,	1769	1615	107	159
Madrid,	Franklin,	404	491	40	52
Manchester,	Kennebec,	New	813	97	37
Mapleton,	Aroostook,	66		41	5
Mariaville,	Hancock,	374	458	38	11
Marion,	Washington,	207	203	15	18
Marshfield,	"	294	328	38	22
Mars Hill plan.,	Aroostook,	29	201	26	19
Masardis,	"	122	190	14	11
Mason,	Oxford,	93	136	15	11
Matinicus Isle,	Knox,	220	276		
Mattamiscontis,	Penobscot,	54	31		
Mattawamkeag,	"		280	6	20
Maxfield,	"	186	162	17	1
Mayfield,	Somerset,	133	118	2	10
Maysville,	Aroostook,	361	665	51	7
Meddybemps,	Washington,	287	297	20	24
Medford,	Piscataquis,	322	353	34	7
Medway plan.,	Penobscot,			32	17
Mercer,	Somerset,	1186	1059	117	54
Merrill plantation,	Aroostook,			13	6
Mexico,	Oxford,	482	671	51	52
Milford,	Penobscot,	687	744	77	24
Millbridge,	Washington,	1170	1282	36	183
Milo,	Piscataquis,	932	959	74	38
Milton,	Oxford,	166	271	u22	24
Minot,	Androscoggin	1734	1799	215	99
Molunkus,	Aroostook,	199	61		
Monhegan Isle,	Lincoln,	103	195		
Monmouth,	Kennebec,	1925	1854	220	120
Monroe,	Waldo,	1606	1703	191	78
Monson,	Piscataquis,	654	708	106	12
Monticello,	Aroostook,	227	483	22	11
Montville,	Waldo,	1881	1682	193	98
Moose River plan.,	Somerset,			8	4
Moro plantation,	Aroostook,			u14	6
Morrill,	Waldo,	New	629	64	55
Moscow,	Somerset,	577	574	40	52
Mt. Chase,	Penobscot,			17	31
Mt. Desert,	Hancock,	782	916	54	52
Mt. Vernon,	Kennebec,	1479	1464	172	55

Town.	County.	1850	1860	Chamb.	Pills.
Muscle Ridge plan.,	Knox,	56	183		
Naples,	Cumberland,	1025	1219	99	120
Newburg,	Penobscot,	1399	1365	127	39
Newcastle,	Lincoln,	2012	1791	228	97
Newfield,	York,	1418	1349	133	155
New Gloucester,	Cumberland,	1848	1654	222	123
New Limerick,	Aroostook,	160	226	18	37
Newport,	Penobscot,	1210	1403	193	102
New Portland,	Somerset,	1460	1554	175	187
Newry,	Oxford,	459	474	28	43
New Sharon,	Franklin,	1732	1731	247	99
New Vineyard,	"	635	864	78	98
Nobleborough,	Lincoln,	1408	1438	121	137
Norridgewock,	Somerset,	1848	1898	126	101
North Berwick,	York,	1593	1492	177	192
Northfield,	Washington,	246	262	16	29
North Haven,	Knox,	806	951	52	48
Northport,	Waldo,	1260	1178	88	92
North Yarmouth,	Cumberland,	1121	1076	123	62
No. 2, R. 2, W.K. R.,	Somerset,		138	15	11
No. 18,	Washington,		40	9	
No. 21,	"		85	5	19
Norway,	Oxford,	1963	1982	234	129
Oakfield,	Aroostook,		New	23	17
Oldtown,	Penobscot,	3087	3860	301	183
Orient,	Aroostook,	207	233	14	10
Orland,	Hancock,	1579	1787	187	107
Orneville,	Piscataquis,	424	512	41	37
Orono,	Penobscot,	2785	2533	191	67
Orrington,	"	1852	1950	145	37
Otis,	Hancock,	124	210	43	7
Otisfield,	Cumberland,	1171	1199	152	106
Oxford,	Oxford,	1233	1281	153	113
Palermo,	Waldo,	1659	1372	136	125
Palmyra,	Somerset,	1625	1597	187	99
Paris,	Oxford,	2882	2827	363	202
Parkman,	Piscataquis,	1243	1166	98	154
Parsonsfield,	York,	2322	2125	257	194
Passadumkeag,	Penobscot,	295	360	22	28
Pattagumpus,	"	50	105	10	
Patten,	"	470	639	81	40
Pembroke,	Washington,	1712	2299	204	196
Penobscot,	Hancock,	1556	1557	92	110
Perham,	Aroostook,			15	
Perkins,	Sagadahoc,	84	95	14	1
Perkins plantation,	Franklin,		118	13	11
Perry,	Washington,	1324	1195	87	55
Peru,	Oxford,	1109	1121	129	46
Phillips,	Franklin,	1673	1698	196	117
Phipsburg,	Sagadahoc,	1805	1770	115	120
Pittsfield,	Somerset,	1166	1495	170	142
Pittston,	Kennebec,	2823	2619	216	263
Pleasant Ridge,	Somerset,			21	7

Town.	County.	1850	1860	Chamb.	Pills.
Plymouth,	Penobscot,	925	989	108	84
Poland,	Androscoggin,	2660	2746	234	162
Porter,	Oxford,	1208	1240	115	110
Portland,	Cumberland,	20815	26341	2046	1325
Pownal,	"	1074	1053	126	113
Prentiss,	Penobscot,		226	22	13
Presque Isle, .	Aroostook,		723	121	7
Princeton,	Washington,	280	626	96	74
Prospect,	Waldo,	2467	1005	43	85
Rangely,	Franklin,		238	31	30
Rangely plan.,	"			6	2
Raymond,	Cumberland,	1192	1229	95	134
Readfield,	Kennebec,	1985	1510	189	82
Reed plantation,	Aroostook,		72		
Richmond,	Sagadahoc,	2056	2739	252	188
Riley plantation,	Oxford,	60	42		
Ripley,	Somerset,	641	655	31	66
Robbinston,	Washington,	1028	1113	70	53
Rockland,	Knox,	5052	7316	656	477
Rome,	Kennebec,	830	864	19	79
Roxbury,	Oxford,	246	251	12	16
Rumford,	"	1375	1375	155	116
Saco,	York,	5798	6223	621	450
Salem,	Franklin,	454	396	32	39
Salmon Brook,	Aroostook,	176	318		
Sandy River,	Franklin,		176	2	9
Sanford,	York,	2330	2273	202	271
Sangerville,	Piscataquis,	1267	1314	90	139
Sarsfield,	Aroostook,	252	473 To Ft. Fairfield		
Scarborough,	Cumberland,	1837	1807	105	228
Searsmont,	Waldo,	1693	1657	145	152
Searsport,	"	2208	2532	215	128
Seaville,	Hancock,	139 To Tremont, Mt. Desert			
Sebago,	Cumberland,	850	958	96	112
Sebec,	Piscataquis,	1223	1152	100	40
Sedgwick,	Hancock,	1235	1263	114	53
Shapleigh,	York,	1348	2221	137	161
Sherman,	Aroostook,			98	30
Shirley,	Piscataquis,	250	282	13	30
Sidney,	Kennebec,	1955	1782	192	156
Skowhegan,	Somerset,	1756	2266	502	183
Smithfield,	"	873	793	90	58
Smyrna,	Aroostook,	172	165	14	2
Solon,	Somerset,	1415	1345	147	131
Somerville,	Lincoln,	552	606	57	61
South Berwick,	York,	2592	2624	232	254
Southport,	Lincoln,	513	708	38	19
South Thomaston,	Knox,	2217	1615	136	110
Springfield,	Penobscot,	583	854	113	37
St. Albans,	Somerset,	1792	1808	202	64
St. George,	Knox,	1420	2716	23	265
Standish,	Cumberland,	2290	2067	240	208
Starks,	Somerset,	1446	1340	119	111

Town.	County.	1850	1860	Chamb.	Pills.
Stetson,	Penobscot,	885	913	100	62
Steuben,	Washington,	1112	1191	110	78
Stockton,	Waldo,	New	1595	198	164
Stoneham,	Oxford,	484	463	41	46
Stow,	"	471	551	47	55
Strong,	Franklin,	1008	754	114	54
Sullivan,	Hancock,	810	862	85	84
Sumner,	Oxford,	1151	1154	153	107
Surry,	Hancock,	1189	1319	78	79
Swan Island,	"	428	492		
Swanville,	Waldo,	944	914	64	62
Sweden,	Oxford,	696	728	75	43
Talmadge plan.,	Washington,			4	10
Temple,	Franklin,	785	726	88	60
Thorndike,	Waldo,	1029	958	118	57
Thomaston,	Knox,	2723	3218	188	311
Topsfield,	Washington,	268	444	33	57
Topsham,	Sagadahoc,	2010	1705	124	126
Tremont,	Hancock,	1425	1708	105	72
Trenton,	"	1205	1400	75	83
Trescott,	Washington,	782	715	15	41
Troy,	Waldo,	1484	1403	114	131
Turner,	Androscoggin,	2536	2682	285	201
Union,	Knox,	1972	1957	209	177
Unity,	Waldo,	1557	1320	154	104
Upton,	Oxford,		219	22	15
Van Buren,	Aroostook,	1050	616	15	76
Vassalborough,	Kennebec,	3099	3181	348	209
Veazie,	Penobscot,	New	893	61	92
Verona,	Hancock,			4	28
Vienna,	Kennebec,	851	878	70	35
Vinalhaven,	Knox,	1252	1667	106	129
Waite,	Washington,	81		3	19
Waldo,	Waldo,	812	728	54	63
Waldoborough,	Lincoln,	4199	4568	258	643
Wales,	Androscoggin,	612	602	68	66
Wallagrass,	Aroostook,			6	13
Waltham	Hancock,	304	374	35	26
Warren,	Knox,	2428	2321	192	267
Washburn,	Aroostook,			21	7
Washington,	Knox,	1756	1662	154	155
Washington plan.,	Franklin,			2	7
Waterborough,	York,	1989	1824	185	236
Waterford,	Oxford,	1448	1407	123	163
Waterville,	Kennebec,	3964	4390	474	209
Wayne,	"	1367	1194	131	46
Webster,	Androscoggin,	1110	890	98	43
Webster plan.,	Penobscot,			4	
Weld,	Franklin,	995	1035	140	84
Wellington,	Piscataquis,	600	694	32	76
Wells,	York,	2945	2878	367	349
Wesley,	Washington,	329	343	33	30
West Bath,	Sagadahoc,	603	400	56	14

Town.	County.	1850	1860	Chamb.	Pills.
Westbrook,	Cumberland,	4852	5113	559	555
Westfield,	Aroostook,		14	8	3
West Forks plan.,	Somerset,			7	5
West Gardiner,	Kennebec,.	New	1294	127	59
Weston,	Aroostook,	293	394	35	35
Westport,	Lincoln,	761	798	29	19
Wetmore Isle,	Hancock,	405	399		
Whitefield,	Lincoln,	2158	1883	197	147
Whiting,	Washington,	470	479	16	40
Whitneyville,	"	519	579	66	55
Williamsburg,	Piscataquis,	124	182	13	7
Wilton,	Franklin,	1909	1920	230	100
Windham,	Cumberland,	2380	2635	298	185
Windsor,	Kennebec,	1793	1548	116	149
Winn,	Penobscot,	New	853	65	34
Winslow,	Kennebec,	1796	1739	156	129
Winterport,	Waldo,	New	2381	305	164
Winthrop,	Kennebec,	2154	2338	325	152
Wiscasset,	Lincoln,	2332	2318	189	220
Woodland,	Aroostook,			11	9
Woodstock.	Oxford,	1012	1025	155	46
Woodville,	Penobscot,		230	6	15
Woolwich,	Sagadahoc,	1420	1317	125	61
Yarmouth,	Cumberland,	2144	2027	202	133
York,	York,	2980	2825	212	290

RECAPITULATION BY COUNTIES.

County.	Population in 1840	1850	1860	Governor, 1867. Chamb.	Pills.
Androscoggin,*			29726	3424	1829
Aroostook,	9413	12529	22479	1582	1146
Cumberland,	68658	79538	75591	7009	5724
Franklin,	20801	20027	20403	2272	1585
Hancock,	28605	34372	37757	2549	1986
Kennebec,	55823	62521	55955	5810	4042
Knox,†			32716	2464	2779
Lincoln,	63517	74875	27860	2279	2274
Oxford,	38351	39763	36698	3829	2997
Penobscot,	45705	63089	72731	6691	4509
Piscataquis,	13138	14735	15032	1490	1004
Sagadahoc,‡			21790	1874	1180
Somerset,	33912	35581	36753	3701	3009
Waldo,	41509	47230	38447	3282	2927
Washington,	28327	38811	42534	2931	2758
York,	54034	60098	62107	6671	6189
	501,793	583,169	628,279	57,332	45,990
				Scattering,	442

*Incorporated in 1854 from parts of Cumberland, Kennebec, Lincoln and Oxford. † Incorporated in 1859 from parts of Lincoln and Waldo. ‡ Incorporated in 1854 from part of Lincoln.

VOTE FOR MEMBERS OF CONGRESS, 1866.

Republican.		Democrat.	
DIS. 1—John Lynch,	15,611	Lorenzo D. M. Sweat,	11,653
2—Sidney Perham,	13,784	Nahum Morrill,	7,363
3—James G. Blaine,	14,909	Solyman Heath,	8,318
4—John A. Peters,	12,059	George M. Weston,	6,564
5—Frederick A. Pike,	12,351	William G. Crosby,	7,973

VOTE OF MAINE SINCE 1854.

Republican.			Democrat.	
1854, Gov.,	Anson P. Morrill,	44,565	Albion K. Parris,	28,462
	Isaac Reed, Whig,	11,001	Shepard Cary,	3,478
1855, "	Anson P. Morrill,	51,441	Samuel Wells,	48,345
			Isaac Reed, Whig,	10,610
1856, "	Hannibal Hamlin,	69,574	Samuel Wells,	43,628
			Geo. F. Patten, Whig,	6,554
1856, Pres.,	John C. Fremont,	67,179	James Buchanan,	39,080
			Mill'rd Filmore, Am.,	3,325
1857, Gov.,	Lot M. Morrill,	54,473	Manasseh H. Smith,	42,940
1858, "	" " "	60,380	" " "	52,440
1859, "	" " "	56,824	" " "	45,318
1860, "	Israel Washburn, jr.,	70,030	Ephraim K. Smart,	52,350
			Phineas Barnes, Bell,	1,735
1860, Pres.,	Abraham Lincoln,	62,811	Stephen A. Douglas,	26,693
	John Bell, Union,	2,046	J. C. Breckinridge,	6,368
1861, Gov.,	Israel Washburn, jr.,	58,689	John W. Dana,	19,801
			Chas. D. Jameson,	21,935
1862, "	Abner Coburn,	46,780	Bion Bradbury,	33,972
			Chas. D. Jameson,	7,696
1863, "	Samuel Cony,	68,339	Bion Bradbury,	50,687
1864, "	" "	65,583	Joseph Howard,	46 403
1864, Pres.,	Abraham Lincoln,	68,114	Geo. B. McClellan,	46,992
1865, Gov.,	Samuel Cony,	54,430	Joseph Howard,	31,609
1866, "	J. L. Chamberlain,	69,637	Eben F. Pillsbury,	41,947
1867, "	" "	57,332	" " "	45,990

Anson P. Morrill was elected by the Legislature Governor for 1855, and Samuel Wells for 1856. At all other elections the Republican candidates had a majority.

EIGHT acres of land in Maine devoted to corn, wheat, rye, oats, barley, buckwheat, potatoes and hay—one acre of each—produced on an average in 1866, crops to the value of $270.97, according to statistics returned to the Agricultural Bureau at Washington; eight acres of the same in Wisconsin yielded crops, in the year named, valued at $190.59. Maine farmers need not go West, or leave the State to improve their condition.

NEW HAMPSHIRE.

Population in 1850 and 1860 by each United States census. Candidates for Governor in 1868: Walter Harriman, Republican; John G. Sinclair, Democrat.

Town.	County.	Population 1850	Population 1860	Governor '68. Harr.	Governor '68. Sinc'r.
Acworth,	Sullivan,	1251	1180	157	135
Albany,	Carroll,	455	430	30	67
Alexandria,	Grafton,	1273	1253	119	138
Allenstown,	Merrimack,	526	414	32	74
Alstead,	Cheshire,	1425	1318	183	145
Alton,	Belknap,	1795	2018	252	231
Amherst,	Hillsborough,	1613	1508	241	124
Andover,	Merrimack,	1220	1243	96	264
Antrim,	Hillsborough,	1143	1123	146	129
Atkinson,	Rockingham,	600	546	85	62
Auburn,	"	810	886	116	97
Barnstead,	Belknap,	1848	1885	116	338
Barrington,	Strafford,	1754	1963	228	204
Bartlett,	Carroll,	761	735	27	145
Bath,	Grafton,	1514	1366	160	164
Bedford,	Hillsborough,	1905	1172	189	132
Bennington,	"	541	450	47	78
Benton,	Grafton,	478	459	16	82
Berlin,	Coos,	173	433	8	59
Bethlehem,	Grafton,	950	896	25	219
Boscawen,	Merrimack,	2063	2274	186	178
Bow,	"	1055	909	96	156
Bradford,	"	1341	1180	122	187
Brentwood,	Rockingham,	923	887	141	69
Bridgewater,	Grafton,	664	560	69	56
Bristol,	"	1103	1124	242	107
Brookfield,	Carroll,	552	510	60	35
Brookline,	Hillsborough,	718	756	115	106
Cambridge,	Coos,	33	49	1	4
Campton,	Grafton,	1439	1320	190	143
Canaan,	"	1683	1762	253	228
Candia,	Rockingham,	1482	1575	217	226
Canterbury,	Merrimack,	1614	1522	133	166
Carroll,	Coos,	299	276	17	70
Centre Harbor,	Belknap,	544	484	60	63
Charlestown,	Sullivan,	1644	1758	232	162
Chatham,	Carroll,	516	489	57	58
Chester,	Rockingham,	1301	1275	208	101
Chesterfield,	Cheshire,	1680	1434	165	164
Chichester,	Merrimack,	997	1041	92	166
Claremont,	Sullivan,	3606	4026	664	284
Clarksville,	Coos,	187	249	18	51
Colebrook,	"	908	1118	144	148
Columbia,	"	762	798	103	75

Town.	County.	1850	1860	Harr.	Sinc'r.
Concord,	Merrimack,	8584	10896	1570	1153
Conway,	Carroll,	1769	1624	183	221
Cornish,	Sullivan,	1606	1520	209	123
Croydon,	"	861	755	98	62
Dalton,	Coos,	750	666	56	102
Danbury,	Grafton,	934	947	88	124
Danville,	Rockingham,	614	620	92	68
Deerfield,	"	2022	2066	233	238
Deering,	Hillsborough,	890	793	74	142
Derry,	Rockingham,	1850	1995	277	161
Dorchester,	Grafton,	711	691	46	106
Dover,	Strafford,	8196	8502	1078	702
Dublin,	Cheshire,	1088	1096	171	77
Dummer,	Coos,	171	289	35	28
Dunbarton,	Merrimack,	915	901	125	84
Durham,	Strafford,	1499	1534	168	210
East Kingston,	Rockingham,	532	598	70	88
Eaton,	Carroll,	1751	780	48	124
Effingham,	"	1252	1209	142	126
Ellsworth,	Grafton,	320	302	12	45
Enfield,	"	1742	1876	251	155
Epping,	Rockingham,	1663	1414	171	198
Epsom,	Merrimack,	1365	1216	108	173
Errol,	Coos,	138	178	6	38
Exeter,	Rockingham,	3329	3309	524	168
Farmington,	Strafford,	1699	2275	306	273
Fitzwilliam,	Cheshire,	1482	1294	223	76
Francestown,	Hillsborough,	1114	1082	175	102
Franconia,	Grafton,	584	708	37	91
Franklin,	Merrimack,	1251	1600	296	245
Freedom,	Carroll,	910	917	44	167
Fremont,	Rockingham,	509	579	82	80
Gilford,	Belknap,	2425	2811	440	354
Gilmanton,	"	3282	2073	246	193
Gilsum,	Cheshire,	666	676	66	95
Goffstown,	Hillsborough,	2270	1740	243	194
Gorham,	Coos,	224	907	88	93
Goshen,	Sullivan,	659	576	51	88
Gosport,	Rockingham,	103	127	12	6
Grafton,	Grafton,	1259	1150	117	158
Grantham,	Sullivan,	784	648	104	76
Greenfield,	Hillsborough,	716	692	54	103
Greenland,	Rockingham,	739	762	92	110
Groton,	Grafton,	776	778	81	80
Hampstead,	Rockingham,	789	930	144	101
Hampton,	"	1197	1230	184	133
Hampton Falls,	"	640	621	95	48
Hancock,	Hillsborough,	1012	844	119	112
Hanover,	Grafton,	2352	2308	310	200
Hart's Location,	Carroll,		44	5	3
Haverhill,	Grafton,	2405	2291	242	322
Hebron,	"	565	475	42	69
Henniker,	Merrimack,	1690	1500	196	172

Town.	County.	1850	1860	Harr.	Sinc'r.
Hill,	Grafton,	951	918	115	85
Hillsboro',	Hillsborough,	1685	1623	183	268
Hinsdale,	Cheshire,	1903	1312	222	100
Holderness,	Grafton,	1744	1705	255	221
Hollis,	Hillsborough,	1293	1317	179	158
Hooksett,	Merrimack,	1503	1257	157	135
Hopkinton,	"	2169	2178	260	242
Hudson,	Hillsborough,	1312	1222	158	146
Jackson,	Carroll,	589	631	6	135
Jaffrey,	Cheshire,	1497	1453	203	133
Jefferson,	Coos,	629	700	50	154
Keene,	Cheshire,	3392	4320	788	435
Kensington,	Rockingham,	700	672	83	94
Kingston,	"	1192	1216	129	146
Laconia,	Belknap,	fr. Meredith	1806	188	255
Lancaster,	Coos,	1559	2020	316	200
Landaff,	Grafton,	948	1012	49	186
Langdon,	Sullivan,	575	478	79	50
Lebanon,	Grafton,	2136	2322	469	208
Lee,	Strafford,	863	871	81	117
Lempster,	Sullivan,	906	820	78	97
Lincoln,	Grafton,	57	71	7	7
Lisbon,	"	1882	1886	253	235
Litchfield,	Hillsborough,	447	352	39	66
Littleton,	Grafton,	2008	2292	238	391
Londonderry,	Rockingham,	1731	1717	229	154
Loudon,	Merrimack,	1553	1638	135	239
Lyman,	Grafton,	1442	743	94	73
Lyme,	"	1618	1572	261	124
Lyndeboro',	Hillsborough,	968	823	119	111
Madbury,	Strafford,	484	496	57	50
Madison,	Carroll,	fr. Eaton	826	113	34
Manchester,	Hillsborough,	13933	20107	2014	1787
Marlboro',	Cheshire,	886	915	196	37
Marlow,	"	708	813	86	116
Mason,	Hillsborough,	1226	1559	190	140
Meredith,	Belknap,	3521	1944	241	260
Merrimack,	Hillsborough,	1250	1119	144	139
Middleton,	Strafford,	476	530	44	71
Milan,	Coos,	493	789	99	70
Milford,	Hillsborough,	2159	2223	438	165
Milton,	Strafford,	1619	1862	202	124
Monroe,	Grafton,	fr. Lyman	619	81	41
Moultonboro',	Carroll,	1748	1448	121	213
Mont Vernon,	Hillsborough,	722	725	85	99
Nashua,	"	*8942	10065	1132	961
Nelson,	Cheshire,	751	699	106	64
New Boston,	Hillsborough,	1476	1369	135	214
Newbury,	Merrimack,	738	698	54	118
Newcastle,	Rockingham,	891	692	92	96
New Durham,	Strafford,	1048	1173	61	190

* Including Nashville, since annexed.

Town.	County.	1850	1860	Harr.	Sinc'r.
New Hampton,	Belknap,	1612	1596	187	120
New Ipswich,	Hillsborough,	1877	1701	199	81
Newington,	Rockingham,	472	475	45	72
New London,	Merrimack,	945	952	152	94
Newmarket,	Rockingham,	1939	2034	185	227
Newport,	Sullivan,	2020	2077	292	270
Newton,	Rockingham,	685	850	97	124
Northfield,	Merrimack,	1332	1051	96	141
North Hampton,	Rockingham,	822	771	87	128
Northumberland,	Coos,	429	736	72	121
Northwood,	Rockingham,	1308	1502	204	149
Nottingham,	"	1268	1297	142	160
Orange,	Grafton,	451	382	54	27
Orford,	"	1406	1255	164	136
Ossipee,	Carroll,	2122	1997	216	270
Pelham,	Hillsborough,	1071	944	108	132
Pembroke,	Merrimack,	1732	1313	198	243
Peterboro',	Hillsborough,	2222	2265	351	190
Piermont,	Grafton,	948	949	110	97
Pittsburg,	Coos,	425	413	57	48
Pittsfield,	Merrimack,	1828	1838	221	228
Plainfield,	Sullivan,	1392	1620	189	198
Plaistow,	Rockingham,	748	861	104	66
Plymouth,	Grafton,	1290	1407	173	176
Portsmouth,	Rockingham,	9739	9335	1180	1122
Randolph,	Coos,	113	118	8	32
Raymond,	Rockingham,	1256	1269	129	197
Richmond,	Cheshire,	1128	1015	104	122
Rindge,	"	1274	1231	215	41
Rochester,	Strafford,	3006	3384	501	410
Rollinsford,	"	1862	2069	199	90
Roxbury,	Cheshire,	260	212	36	10
Rumney,	Grafton,	1109	1103	142	146
Rye,	Rockingham,	1296	1199	92	212
Salem,	"	1555	1670	227	204
Salisbury,	Merrimack,	1228	1191	94	153
Sanbornton,	Belknap,	2695	2743	266	366
Sandown,	Rockingham,	566	553	60	88
Sandwich,	Carroll,	2577	2227	312	227
Seabrook,	Rockingham,	1296	1549	187	189
Sharon,	Hillsborough,	226	250	23	26
Shelburne,	Coos,	480	318	42	29
Somersworth,	Strafford,	4943	4787	625	288
South Hampton,	Rockingham,	472	549	63	68
South Newmarket,	"	516	786	181	40
Springfield,	Sullivan,	1270	1021	105	125
Stark,	Coos,	418	426	29	85
Stewartstown,	"	747	771	47	145
Stoddard,	Cheshire,	1105	944	81	129
Strafford,	Strafford,	1920	2047	217	276
Stratford,	Coos,	552	716	71	109
Stratham,	Rockingham,	843	859	130	80
Sullivan,	Cheshire,	468	376	55	29

Town.	County.	1850	1860	Harr.	Sinc'r.
Snnapee,	Sullivan,	787	778	61	148
Surry,	Cheshire,	556	389	50	44
Sutton,	Merrimack,	1387	1431	155	151
Swanzey,	Cheshire.	2106	1798	180	248
Tamworth,	Carroll,	1766	1678	212	146
Temple,	Hillsborough,	579	501	64	70
Thornton,	Grafton,	1012	967	58	152
Troy,	Cheshire,	759	761	94	79
Tuftonboro',	Carroll,	1305	1186	*90	*169
Unity,	Sullivan,	961	887	57	162
Upper Gilmanton,	Belknap, fr. Gilmanton	1189		103	175
Wakefield,	Carroll,	1405	1478	175	165
Walpole,	Cheshire,	2034	1868	215	211
Warner,	Merrimack,	2038	1970	222	274
Warren,	Grafton,	872	1152	42	196
Washington,	Sullivan,	1054	897	118	117
Waterville,	Grafton,	40	48	2	11
Weare,	Hillsborough,	2436	2310	314	260
Webster,	Merrimack, fr. Boscawen			111	82
Wentworth,	Grafton,	1197	1055	82	177
" Locat'n,	Coos,		57		14
Westmoreland,	Cheshire,	1677	1285	164	143
Whitefield,	Coos,	857	1015	123	139
Wilmot,	Merrimack,	1272	1195	113	182
Wilton,	Hillsborough,	1161	1369	190	253
Winchester,	Cheshire,	3296	2225	273	210
Windham,	Rockingham,	818	846	141	63
Windsor,	Hillsborough,	172	136	8	20
Wolfboro',	Carroll,	1405	2300	282	302
Woodstock,	Grafton,	418	476	30	69

RECAPITULATION BY COUNTIES.

	Population in			Governor, 1868.	
Counties.	1840	1850	1860	Harr.	Sinc'r.
Belknap,†	New	17721	18549	2099	2355
Carroll,†	"	20157	20465	2033	2438
Cheshire,	26429	30144	27434	3876	2708
Coos,	9849	11853	13161	1390	1814
Grafton,	42311	42342	42260	4979	5245
Hillsborough,	42494	57478	62140	7476	6508
Merrimack,	36253	40337	41408	5020	5300
Rockingham,	45771	49194	50122	6530	5626
Strafford,	61127	29374	31493	3827	3005
Sullivan,	20340	19375	19041	2494	2097
	284,574	317,976	326,073	39,724	37,098
				Scattering,	28

* Unofficial. † Incorporated from Strafford.

VOTE OF NEW HAMPSHIRE SINCE 1855.

Republican.			*Democratic.*	
1855, Gov., Ralph Metcalf, Am.,	32,769	Nath'l B. Baker,	27,055
James Bell, Whig,	3,436	Asa Fowler, Free S.,	1,237
1856, " Ralph Metcalf,	32,119	John S. Wells,	32,031
Ichabod Goodwin,W.,	2,360		
1856, Pres., John C. Fremont,	38,345	James Buchanan,	32,789
		Mill'd Fillmore, Am.,	422
1857, Gov., William Haile,	34,216	John S. Wells,	31,214
1858, " " "	36,215	Asa P. Cate,	31,679
1859, " Ichabod Goodwin,	36,326	" " "	32,802
1860, " " "	38,037	" " "	33,544
1860, Pres., Abraham Lincoln,	37,519	Stephen A. Douglas,	25,881
John Bell, Union,	441	J. C. Breckinridge,	2,112
1861, Gov., Nathaniel S. Berry,	35,467	George Stark,	31,452
1862 " " " "	32,150	" " "	28,566
		Paul J. Wheeler,	1,709
1863, " Joseph A. Gilmore,	29,035	Ira A. Eastman,	32,833
W. Harriman,War D.,	4,372		
1864, " Joseph A. Gilmore,	37,006	Ed. W. Harrington,	31,340
1864, Pres., Abraham Lincoln,	36,400	Geo. B. McClellan,	32,871
1865, Gov., Frederick Smyth,	34,145	Ed. W. Harrington,	28,017
1866, " " "	35,136	John G. Sinclair,	30,484
1867, " Walter Harriman,	35,809	" " "	32,663
1868, " " "	39,724	" " "	37,098

The Republican candidates for Governor when not receiving a majority vote have been elected by the Legislature.

VOTE FOR MEMBERS OF CONGRESS, 1867.

Republican.		*Democratic.*	
Dis. 1—Jacob H. Ela,	13,243	Daniel Marcy,	12,247
2—Aaron F. Stevens,	11,260	Edward W. Harrington,	10,305
3—Jacob Benton,	11,294	Harry Bingham,	10,246

Gov. Harriman in his last message, says that the people of New Hampshire probably consume about a barrel of flour a year, each, at a cost of $6,000,000. He believes that wheat enough can be raised in the State for the use of its people. Three acres of wheat to each farm would be 90,000 acres, and a yield of fifteen bushels per acre would give 1,350,000 bushels, enough to make 300,000 barrels of flour, or nearly one to each person.

VERMONT.

Population in 1850 and 1860 by each United States census. Candidates for Governor in 1867: John B. Page, Republican; John L. Edwards, Democrat.

Town.	County.	Population 1850	Population 1860	Governor '68. Page.	Governor '68. Edws.
Addison,	Addison,	1279	1000	76	
Albany,	Orleans,	1052	1224	97	29
Alburgh,	Grand Isle,	1568	1793	126	39
Andover,	Windsor,	725	670	67	
Arlington,	Bennington,	1084	1146	224	59
Athens,	Windham,	359	382	48	22
Averill,	Essex,	7	12		
Bakersfield,	Franklin,	1523	1451	127	101
Baltimore,	Windsor,	124	116	15	
Barnard,	"	1647	1487	172	118
Barnet,	Caledonia,	2521	1994	133	64
Barre,	Washington,	1845	1839	169	47
Barton,	Orleans,	987	1590	125	59
Belvidere,	Lamoille,	256	366	31	29
Bennington,	Bennington,	3923	4389	760	281
Benson,	Rutland,	1305	1256	108	1
Berkshire,	Franklin,	1955	1890	83	19
Berlin,	Washington,	1507	1545	121	69
Bethel,	Windsor,	1730	1804	115	69
Bloomfield,	Essex,	244	320	37	34
Bolton,	Chittenden,	602	645	50	38
Bradford,	Orange,	1723	1689	197	192
Braintree,	"	1228	1225	136	40
Brandon,	Rutland,	2835	3077	341	184
Brattleboro',	Windham,	3816	3855	366	44
Bridgewater,	Windsor,	1311	1292	120	129
Bridport,	Addison,	1393	1298	146	16
Brighton,	Essex,	193	945	108	70
Bristol,	Addison,	1344	1355	148	35
Brookfield,	Orange,	1672	1521	129	45
Brookline,	Windham,	285	243	29	8
Brownington,	Orleans,	613	761	64	5
Brunswick,	Essex,	119	212	8	17
Burke,	Caledonia,	1103	1138	116	30
Burlington,	Chittenden,	7585	7713	548	263
Cabot,	Washington,	1356	1318	131	73
Calais,	"	1410	1409	112	76
Cambridge,	Lamoille,	1849	1784	113	68
Canaan,	Essex,	471	412	40	25
Castleton,	Rutland,	3016	2852	173	27
Cavendish,	Windsor,	1576	1509	116	27
Charleston,	Orleans,	1008	1160	154	22
Charlotte,	Chittenden,	1634	1589	150	15

Town.	County.	1850	1860	Page.	Edws.
Chelsea,	Orange,	1958	1757	199	56
Chester,	Windsor,	2001	2126	250	30
Chittenden,	Rutland,	675	763	45	7
Clarendon,	"	1477	1237	110	4
Colchester,	Chittenden,	2575	3041	201	214
Concord,	Essex,	1153	1291	144	31
Corinth,	Orange,	1906	1627	182	191
Cornwall,	Addison,	1155	977	146	*3
Coventry,	Orleans,	867	914	95	17
Craftsbury,	"	1223	1413	121	32
Danby,	Rutland,	1535	1419	134	23
Danville,	Caledonia,	2577	2544	136	220
Derby,	Orleans,	1750	1906	113	49
Dorset,	Bennington,	1700	2090	204	211
Dover,	Windham,	709	650	56	15
Dummerston,	"	1645	1021	100	15
Duxbury,	Washington,	845	1000	53	11
East Haven,	Essex,	94	136	37	10
East Montpelier,	Washington,	1447	1328	176	39
Eden,	Lamoille,	668	919	95	25
Elmore,	"	504	602	65	26
Enosburgh,	Franklin,	2009	2066	176	18
Essex,	Chittenden,	2052	1906	207	91
Fairfax,	Franklin,	2111	1987	213	36
Fairfield,	"	2591	2497	131	158
Fairhaven,	Rutland,	902	1378	169	18
Fairlee,	Orange,	575	549	66	38
Fayston,	Washington,	684	800	54	18
Ferdinand,	Essex,		34		
Ferrisburgh,	Addison,	2075	1738	147	3
Fletcher,	Franklin,	1084	916	76	83
Franklin,	"	1646	1781	149	21
Georgia,	"	2686	1547	106	9
Glastenbury,	Bennington,	52	47	5	18
Glover,	Orleans,	1137	1244	100	49
Goshen,	Addison,	486	394	63	1
Grafton,	Windham,	1241	1154	151	30
Granby,	Essex,	127	132	23	12
Grand Isle,	Grand Isle,	666	708	70	21
Granville,	Addison,	603	720	59	12
Greensboro',	Orleans,	1008	1065	80	43
Groton,	Caledonia,	895	939	95	17
Guildhall,	Essex,	501	552	68	38
Guilford,	Windham,	1389	1291	78	18
Halifax,	"	1133	1126	*77	*24
Hancock,	Addison,	430	448	82	8
Hardwick,	Caledonia,	1402	1369	169	43
Hartford,	Windsor,	2159	2396	184	20
Hartland,	"	2063	1748	138	38
Highgate,	Franklin,	2653	2526	167	110

* Scattering.

Town.	County.	1850	1860	Page.	Edrs.
Hinesburgh,	Chittenden,	1834	1702	198	12
Holland,	Orleans,	669	748	71	90
Hubbardton,	Rutland,	701	606	32	18
Huntington,	Chittenden,	885	862	163	14
Hyde Park,	Lamoille,	1107	1409	153	143
Ira,	Rutland,	400	422	54	
Irasburgh,	Orleans,	1034	1131	147	3
Isle La Motte,	Grand Isle,	476	564	45	32
Jamaica,	Windham,	1606	1541	139	14
Jay,	Orleans,	371	474	76	15
Jericho,	Chittenden,	1837	1669	202	49
Johnson,	Lamoille,	1381	1526	125	21
Kirby,	Caledonia,	509	473	*38	*14
Landgrove,	Bennington,	337	320	65	6
Leicester,	Addison,	596	737	73	24
Lemington,	Essex,	187	207	17	21
Lincoln,	Addison,	1057	1070	119	
Londonderry,	Windham,	1274	1367	177	40
Lowell,	Orleans,	637	813	85	56
Ludlow,	Windsor,	1619	1568	217	39
Lunenburgh,	Essex,	1123	1034	112	32
Lyndon,	Caledonia,	1752	1695	254	213
Maidstone,	Essex,	237	259	19	31
Manchester,	Bennington,	1782	1688	307	49
Marlboro,'	Windham,	896	741	64	16
Marshfield,	Washington,	1102	1160	124	70
Mendon,	Rutland,	504	633	61	42
Middlebury,	Addison,	3517	2879	224	39
Middlesex,	Washington,	1365	1254	132	66
Middletown,	Rutland,	875	712	108	24
Milton,	Chittenden,	2451	1963	291	66
Monktown,	Addison,	1246	1123	238	12
Montgomery,	Franklin,	1001	1262	141	8
Montpelier,	Washington,	2310	2411	288	112
Moretown,	"	1335	1410	58	107
Morgan,	Orleans,	486	548	77	7
Morristown,	Lamoille,	1441	1751	168	32
Mt. Holly,	Rutland,	1534	1522	101	8
Mt. Tabor,	"	308	358	46	
Newark,	Caledonia,	434	567	64	56
Newbury,	Orange,	2984	2549	248	156
Newfane,	Windham,	1304	1192	125	45
New Haven,	Addison,	1663	1419	142	7
Newport,	Orleans,	748	1197	190	60
Northfield,	Washington,	2922	4329	359	240
North Hero,	Grand Isle,	730	594	61	29
Norton,	Essex,		32		
Norwich,	Windsor,	1978	1759	171	93
Orange,	Orange,	1007	936	69	25
Orwell,	Addison,	1470	1341	103	14
Panton,	"	559	511	53	

* Unofficial.

Town.	County.	1850	1860	Page.	Edws.
Pawlet,	Rutland,	1843	1539	158	58
Peacham,	Caledonia,	1377	1247	164	30
Peru,	Bennington,	567	543	68	18
Pittsfield,	Rutland,	512	493	66	2
Pittsford,	"	2026	1839	142	28
Plainfield,	Washington,	808	822	54	74
Plymouth,	Windsor,	1226	1252	80	
Pomfret,	"	1546	1376	118	26
Poultney,	Rutland,	2329	2278	184	1
Pownal,	Bennington,	1742	1731	261	98
Putney,	Windham,	1425	1163	*152	*28
Randolph,	Orange,	2666	2502	423	71
Reading,	Windsor,	1171	1159	143	13
Readsboro',	Bennington,	857	930	101	66
Richford,	Franklin,	1074	1338	167	42
Richmond,	Chittenden,	1453	1400	151	39
Ripton,	Addison,	567	570	62	14
Rochester,	Windsor,	1493	1507	234	3
Rockingham,	Windham,	2837	2904	275	192
Roxbury,	Washington,	967	1060	90	71
Royalton,	Windsor,	1850	1739	187	4
Rupert,	Bennington,	1101	1103	119	9
Rutland,	Rutland,	3715	7577	700	389
Ryegate,	Caledonia,	1606	1098	69	43
Salem,	Orleans,	455	603	38	11
Salisbury,	Addison,	1027	853	127	5
Sandgate,	Bennington,	850	805	107	46
Searsburgh,	"	201	262	43	6
Shaftsbury,	"	1896	1936	230	171
Sharon,	Windsor,	1240	1111	114	72
Sheffield,	Caledonia,	797	836	90	96
Shelburne,	Chittenden,	1257	1178	96	13
Sheldon,	Franklin,	1814	1655	125	95
Sherburne,	Rutland,	578	525	60	42
Shoreham,	Addison,	1601	1382	119	1
Shrewsbury,	Rutland,	1268	1175	119	36
Somerset,	Windham,	321	105	11	1
South Burlington,	Chittenden,	fr. Burlington		56	28
South Hero,	Grand Isle,	705	617	65	47
Springfield,	Windsor,	2762	2958	407	34
Stamford,	Bennington,	833	759	51	80
Stannard,	Caledonia,	215	240		
St. Albans,	Franklin,	3567	3637	487	262
St. George,	Chittenden,	127	121	13	11
St. Johnsbury,	Caledonia,	2758	3469	561	96
Starksboro',	Addison,	1400	1437	127	28
Stockbridge,	Windsor,	1327	1264	129	18
Strafford,	Orange,	1540	1506	166	94
Stratton,	Windham,	286	366	37	14
Stowe,	Lamoille,	1771	2046	197	46
Sudbury,	Rutland,	794	696	71	62

*Unofficial.

Town.	County.	1850	1860	Page.	Edws.
Sunderland,	Bennington,	479	567	76	53
Sutton,	Caledonia,	1001	987	115	71
Swanton,	Franklin,	2824	2678	160	96
Thetford,	Orange,	2016	1876	174	99
Tinmouth,	Rutland,	717	620	49	
Topsham,	Orange,	1668	1682	142	100
Townsend,	Windham,	1354	1376	157	28
Troy,	Orleans,	1008	1248	141	81
Tunbridge,	Orange,	1786	1546	132	24
Underhill,	Chittenden,	1599	1637	145	90
Vergennes,	Addison,	1378	1286	128	4
Vernon,	Windham,	821	725	45	3
Vershire,	Orange,	1071	1054	96	108
Victory,	Essex,	168	212	27	19
Waitsfield,	Washington,	1021	1005	84	10
Walden,	Caledonia,	910	1099	107	79
Wallingford,	Rutland,	1688	1747	198	16
Waltham,	Addison,	270	263	35	6
Wardsboro',	Windham,	1125	1004	107	32
Warren,	Washington,	962	1041	141	26
Washington,	Orange,	1348	1249	142	44
Waterbury,	Washington,	2352	2198	237	77
Waterford,	Caledonia,	1412	1171	97	14
Waterville,	Lamoille,	753	747	58	11
Weathersfield,	Windsor,	1851	1765	118	28
Wells,	Rutland,	804	642	*49	*47
Wenlock,	Essex,	26			
West Fairlee,	Orange,	696	830	110	80
Westfield,	Orleans,	502	618	94	17
Westford,	Chittenden,	1458	1231	119	23
West Haven,	Rutland,	718	580	36	4
Westminster,	Windham,	1721	1300	115	31
Westmore,	Orleans,	152	324	49	6
Weston,	Windsor,	950	932	158	
West Windsor,	"	1002	924	67	
Weybridge,	Addison,	804	667	78	11
Wheelock,	Caledonia,	855	832	96	63
Whiting,	Addison,	629	542	58	12
Whitingham,	Windham,	1380	1372	112	100
Williamstown,	Orange,	1452	1377	117	43
Williston,	Chittenden,	1669	1479	187	
Wilmington,	Windham,	1372	1424	143	88
Windham,	"	763	680	93	5
Windsor,	Windsor,	1928	1669	173	43
Winhall,	Bennington,	762	741	98	23
Wolcott,	Lamoille,	909	1161	119	39
Woodbury,	Washington,	1070	999	82	17
Woodford,	Bennington,	423	379	54	50
Woodstock,	Windsor,	3041	3062	380	28
Worcester,	Washington,	702	684	86	38

* Unofficial.

RECAPITULATION BY COUNTIES.

County.	Population in 1840	1850	1860	Governor, 1867. Page.	Edws.
Addison,	23583	26549	24010	2553	252
Bennington,	16872	18589	19436	2773	1244
Caledonia,	21891	23595	21708	2266	1135
Chittenden,	22977	29036	28171	2777	986
Essex,	4226	4650	5786	640	340
Franklin,	24531	28586	27231	2308	1058
Grand Isle,	3883	4145	4276	367	167
Lamoille,	10475	10872	12311	1124	435
Orange,	27873	27296	25455	2728	1406
Orleans,	13634	15707	18981	1917	659
Rutland,	30699	33059	35946	3265	993
Washington,	23506	24654	27612	2551	1241
Windham,	27442	29062	26982	2428	761
Windsor,	40356	38320	37193	3997	832
	291,948	314,120	315,098	31,694	11,510
			Scattering,		22

VOTE OF VERMONT SINCE 1856.

Republican.		Democratic.	
1856, Gov., Ryland Fletcher,	34,757	Henry Keyes,	11,747
1856, Pres., John C. Fremont,	39,563	James Buchanan,	10,569
		Mill'd Fillmore, Am.,	545
1857, Gov., Ryland Fletcher,	26,992	Henry Keyes,	12,943
1858, " Hiland Hall,	29,660	" "	13,338
1859, " " "	31,045	John G. Saxe,	14,328
1860, " Erastus Fairbanks,	34,260	" " "	11,890
1860, Pres., Abraham Lincoln,	33,808	Stephen A. Douglas,	6,849
John Bell, Union,	1,969	J. C. Breckinridge,	218
1861, Gov., Frederick Holbrook,	33,152	Daniel A. Smalley,	3,190
		Andrew Tracy, Un.,	5,722
1862, " " "	30,032	Daniel A. Smalley,	3,724
1863, " John G. Smith,	29,228	Timothy P. Redfield,	11,917
1864, " " " "	31,260	" " "	12,283
1864, Pres., Abraham Lincoln,	42,419	Geo. B. McClellan,	13,321
1865, Gov., Paul Dillingham,	27,586	Chas. N. Davenport,	8,857
1866, " " "	34,117	" " "	11,292
1867, " John B. Page,	31,694	John L. Edwards,	11,510

VOTE FOR MEMBERS OF CONGRESS, 1866.

Republican.		Democratic.	
Dis. 1—Fred'k E. Woodbridge,	10,568	Samuel Wells,	3,036
2—Luke P. Poland,	10,844	Charles M. Chase,	3,935
3—Worthington C. Smith,	5,730	Waldo Brigham,	2,680
Asa O. Aldis,	2,794		

MASSACHUSETTS.

Population by each National census of 1850 and 1860, and by the State census of 1865. Candidates for Governor in 1867: Alexander H. Bullock, Republican; John Quincy Adams, Democrat.

		Population in			Governor '67.	
Town.	*County.*	**1850**	**1860**	**1865**	*Bull'k.*	*Adams*
Abington,	Plymouth,	5269	8527	8576	1023	526
Acton,	Middlesex,	1605	1726	1660	155	173
Acushnet,	Bristol, fr. Fairhaven	1387	1251	109	29	
Adams,	Berkshire,	6172	6924	8298	731	321
Agawam,	Hampden,	*	1698	1664	85	123
Alford,	Berkshire,	502	542	461	34	67
Amesbury,	Essex,	3143	3877	4181	397	334
Amherst,	Hampshire,	3057	3206	3415	485	159
Andover,	Essex,	6945	4765	5314	436	224
Arlington,	Middlesex,	2202	2681	2760	191	213
Ashburnham,	Worcester,	1875	2108	2153	253	130
Ashby,	Middlesex,	1208	1091	1080	150	67
Ashfield,	Franklin,	1394	1302	1221	172	39
Ashland,	Middlesex,	1304	1554	1702	213	131
Athol,	Worcester,	2034	2604	2814	291	86
Attleboro',	Bristol,	4200	6066	6200	453	279
Auburn,	Worcester,	879	914	959	85	38
Barnstable,	Barnstable,	4901	5129	4928	285	244
Barre,	Worcester,	2976	2973	2856	214	238
Becket,	Berkshire,	1223	1578	1393	91	61
Bedford,	Middlesex,	975	843	820	86	62
Belchertown,	Hampshire,	2680	2709	2636	244	63
Bellingham,	Norfolk,	1281	1313	1240	124	69
Belmont,	Middlesex,	†	1198	1279	101	67
Berkley,	Bristol,	908	825	847	79	21
Berlin,	Worcester,	866	1106	1061	137	35
Bernardston,	Franklin,	937	968	902	110	60
Beverly,	Essex,	5376	6154	5942	558	265
Billerica,	Middlesex,	1646	1776	1808	210	72
Blackstone,	Worcester,	4391	5453	4857	259	200
Blandford,	Hampden,	1418	1256	1087	89	104
Bolton,	Worcester,	1263	1348	1502	236	37
Boston,	Suffolk,	136881	177818	192318	7322	9064
" with Roxbury,		155245	202955	220744	8457	11050
Boxboro',	Middlesex,	395	403	454	33	48
Boxford,	Essex,	982	1020	868	91	77
Boylston,	Worcester,	918	929	792	133	14
Bradford,	Essex,	1328	1688	1566	145	100
Braintree,	Norfolk,	2069	3468	3725	291	329
Brewster,	Barnstable,	1525	1489	1456	93	30

* From West Springfield. † From Arlington, Watertown and Waltham.

Town.	County.	1850	1860	1865	Bull'k.	Adams
Bridgewater,	Plymouth,	2790	3761	4196	228	249
Brighton,	Middlesex,	2356	3375	3854	189	433
Brimfield,	Hampden,	1420	1363	1316	129	64
Brookfield,	Worcester,	1674	2276	2101	296	96
Brookline,	Norfolk,	2516	5164	5267	342	229
Buckland,	Franklin,	1056	1702	1922	136	58
Burlington,	Middlesex,	545	606	594	25	75
Cambridge,	"	15215	26060	29112	1785	1801
Canton,	Norfolk,	2598	3242	3318	239	263
Carlisle,	Middlesex,	632	621	642	69	45
Carver,	Plymouth,	1186	1186	1059	98	100
Charlemont,	Franklin,	1173	1075	994	144	22
Charlestown,	Middlesex,	17216	25065	26399	1624	2061
Charlton,	Worcester,	2015	2047	1925	242	113
Chatham,	Barnstable,	2439	2710	2624	99	67
Chelmsford,	Middlesex,	2097	2292	2291	242	123
Chelsea,	Suffolk,	6701	13395	14403	1166	702
Cheshire,	Berkshire,	1298	1533	1650	81	192
Chester,	Hampden,	1521	1314	1266	88	100
Chesterfield,	Hampshire,	1014	897	801	116	43
Chicopee,	Hampden,	8291	7261	7577	481	359
Chilmark,	Dukes,	747	654	548	25	31
Clarksburg,	Berkshire,	384	420	530	43	17
Clinton,	Worcester,	3113	3859	4021	339	237
Cohasset,	Norfolk,	1775	1953	2048	138	151
Colerain,	Franklin,	1785	1798	1726	261	35
Concord,	Middlesex,	2249	2246	2232	174	160
Conway,	Franklin,	1831	1689	1538	153	61
Cummington,	Hampshire,	1172	1085	980	173	19
Dalton,	Berkshire,	1020	1243	1137	45	101
Dana,	Worcester,	842	876	789	89	48
Danvers,	Essex,	8109	5110	5144	557	213
Dartmouth,	Bristol,	3868	3883	3435	357	53
Dedham,	Norfolk,	4447	6330	7195	392	480
Deerfield,	Franklin,	2421	3073	3038	242	156
Dennis,	Barnstable,	3257	3662	3592	236	43
Dighton,	Bristol,	1641	1733	1813	188	48
Dorchester,	Norfolk,	7969	9769	10717	773	633
Douglas,	Worcester,	1878	2442	2155	143	161
Dover,	Norfolk,	631	679	616	57	70
Dracut,	Middlesex,	3503	*1881	1905	136	119
Dudley,	Worcester,	1443	1736	2076	117	121
Dunstable,	Middlesex,	590	487	533	41	67
Duxbury,	Plymouth,	2679	2597	2384	196	166
E.Bridgewater,	"	2545	3207	2976	337	274
Eastham,	Barnstable,	845	779	757	37	22
Easthampton,	Hampshire,	1342	1916	2869	267	58
Easton,	Bristol,	2337	3067	3076	254	102
Edgartown,	Dukes,	1990	2118	1846	127	43
Egremont,	Berkshire,	1013	1079	928	116	88

* Part annexed to Lowell in 1851.

Town.	County.	1850	1860	1865	Bull'k.	Adams
Enfield,	Hampshire,	1036	1025	997	122	28
Erving,	Franklin,	449	527	576	88	7
Essex,	Essex,	1585	1701	1630	210	65
Fairhaven,	Bristol,	4304	3118	2547	286	31
Fall River,	"	11524	14026	17481	1662	785
Falmouth,	Barnstable,	2621	2456	2283	199	65
Fitchburg,	Worcester,	5120	7805	8118	1077	462
Florida,	Berkshire,	561	645	1173	65	10
Foxborough,	Norfolk,	1880	2879	2778	403	44
Framingham,	Middlesex,	4252	4227	4665	426	230
Franklin,	Norfolk,	1818	2172	2510	272	103
Freetown,	Bristol,	1615	1521	1485	127	71
Gardner,	Worcester,	1533	2646	2553	297	260
Georgetown,	Essex,	2052	2075	1926	203	201
Gill,	Franklin,	754	683	635	56	52
Gloucester,	Essex,	7786	10904	11937	916	398
Goshen,	Hampshire,	512	439	411	67	6
Gosnold,	Dukes,	fr. Chilmark		108	7	
Grafton,	Worcester,	3904	4317	3961	338	231
Granby,	Hampshire,	1104	907	908	138	18
Granville,	Hampden,	1305	1385	1367	67	152
Gr. Barrington,	Berkshire,	3264	3871	3920	372	212
Greenfield,	Franklin,	2580	3198	3211	315	180
Greenwich,	Hampshire,	838	699	648	59	78
Groton,	Middlesex,	2515	3193	3176	366	106
Groveland,	Essex,	1286	1448	1619	188	154
Hadley,	Hampshire,	1986	2105	2246	269	52
Halifax,	Plymouth,	784	766	722	75	71
Hamilton,	Essex,	889	789	799	62	75
Hancock,	Berkshire,	789	857	837	63	36
Hanover,	Plymouth,	1592	1565	1545	225	62
Hanson,	"	1217	1245	1196	127	109
Hardwick,	Worcester,	1631	1521	1967	111	134
Harvard,	"	1630	1507	1355	136	118
Harwich,	Barnstable,	3258	3423	3540	196	34
Hatfield,	Hampshire,	1073	1337	1405	169	28
Haverhill,	Essex,	5877	9995	10740	1183	782
Hawley,	Franklin,	881	671	687	73	6
Heath,	"	803	661	642	65	15
Hingham,	Plymouth,	3980	4351	4176	382	255
Hinsdale,	Berkshire,	1253	1470	1517	137	112
Holden,	Worcester,	1933	1945	1846	179	89
Holland,	Hampden,	449	419	368	39	15
Holliston,	Middlesex,	2428	3339	3125	318	278
Holyoke,	Hampden,	3245	4997	5648	253	291
Hopkinton,	Middlesex,	2801	4340	4132	279	259
Hubbardston,	Worcester,	1825	1621	1546	171	128
Hudson,	Middlesex,	fr. Marlboro' & Stow			186	122
Hull,	Plymouth,	253	285	260	15	27
Huntington,	Hampshire,	756	1216	1163	92	80
Hyde Park,	Norfolk, Inc. '68 fr. Dorchester, Milton and Dedham					
Ipswich,	Essex,	3349	3300	3311	212	299
Kingston,	Plymouth,	1591	1655	1626	150	126

Town.	County.	1850	1860	1865	Bull'k.	Adams
Lakeville,	Plym'th, fr. Middleboro'	1160	1110	181	38	
Lancaster,	Worcester,	1688	1932	1752	245	42
Lanesborough,	Berkshire,	1229	1308	1294	76	89
Lawrence,	Essex,	8282	17639	21698	1250	1211
Lee,	Berkshire,	3220	4420	4035	275	280
Leicester,	Worcester,	2269	2748	2527	269	125
Lenox,	Berkshire,	1599	1711	1660	114	139
Leominster,	Worcester,	3121	3522	3313	646	60
Leverett,	Franklin,	948	964	914	99	61
Lexington,	Middlesex,	1893	2328	2220	159	155
Leyden,	Franklin,	716	606	592	50	29
Lincoln,	Middlesex,	719	717	711	82	21
Littleton	"	987	1059	967	98	47
Longmeadow,	Hampden,	1252	1376	1480	146	55
Lowell,	Middlesex,	33383	36827	*30990	2395	1598
Ludlow,	Hampden,	1186	1174	1232	91	67
Lunenburg,	Worcester,	1249	1212	1167	172	66
Lynn,	Essex,	14257	19083	20717	1858	1473
Lynnfield,	"	1723	866	725	57	63
Malden,	Middlesex,	3520	5847	6840	608	407
Manchester,	Essex,	1638	1698	1643	203	93
Mansfield,	Bristol,	1789	2114	2130	254	79
Marblehead,	Essex,	6167	7646	7308	†376	542
Marion,	Plymouth, fr. Rochester	918	960	102	36	
Marlborough,	Middlesex,	2941	5907	7164	438	458
Marshfield,	Plymouth,	1837	1870	1809	155	89
Mattapoisett,	" fr. Rochester	1483	1451	176	7	
Medfield,	Norfolk,	966	1082	1012	130	61
Medford,	Middlesex,	3749	4831	4839	546	341
Medway,	Norfolk,	2778	3195	3219	452	146
Melrose,	Middlesex,	1260	2527	2865	330	126
Mendon,	Worcester,	1300	1351	1207	116	59
Methuen,	Essex,	2538	2566	2576	259	235
Middleboro',	Plymouth,	5336	4553	4566	487	298
Middlefield,	Hampshire,	737	748	727	64	12
Middleton,	Essex,	832	940	922	84	48
Milford,	Worcester,	4819	9132	9108	743	456
Millbury,	"	3081	3296	3780	336	129
Milton,	Norfolk,	2241	2669	2770	164	182
Monroe,	Franklin,	254	236	191	26	
Monson,	Hampden,	2831	3164	3272	176	175
Montague,	Franklin,	1518	1593	1574	238	54
Monterey,	Berkshire,	761	758	737	70	57
Montgomery,	Hampden,	393	371	353	17	41
Mt. Wash'ton,	Berkshire,	351	321	237	19	7
Nahant,	Essex, fr. Lynn	380	313	29	25	
Nantucket,	Nantucket,	8452	6094	4748	321	40
Natick,	Middlesex,	2744	5487	5208	509	420
Needham,	Norfolk,	1944	2658	2793	173	159
New Ashford,	Berkshire,	186	239	178	13	19
New Bedford,	Bristol,	16443	22300	20853	1997	602

*January, 1866, it was 36,878. † 78 for R. C. Pitman.

Town.	County.	1850	1860	1865	Bull'k.	Adams
New Braintree,	Worcester,	852	805	752	51	40
Newbury,	Essex,	4426	*1444	1362	83	104
Newburyport,	"	9572	13401	12976	547	1190
New Marlboro',	Berkshire,	1847	1782	1649	156	145
New Salem,	Franklin,	1253	957	1116	126	51
Newton,	Middlesex,	5258	8375	8975	805	475
Northampton,	Hampshire,	5278	6788	7925	782	272
North Andov'r,	Essex, fr. Andover	2343	2622	166	273
Northboro',	Worcester,	1535	1565	1623	146	131
Northbridge,	"	2230	2633	2642	203	160
N. Bridgewat'r,	Plymouth,	3939	6584	6332	782	398
N. Brookfield,	Worcester	1939	2760	2514	249	184
North Chelsea,	Suffolk,	935	921	858	45	77
Northfield,	Franklin,	1772	1712	1660	133	135
North Reading,	Middlesex, fr. Reading	1203	987	104	72
Norton,	Bristol,	1966	1848	1709	185	98
Oakham,	Worcester,	1137	959	925	76	55
Orange,	Franklin,	1701	1622	1909	309	72
Orleans,	Barnstable,	1848	1678	1585	147	75
Otis,	Berkshire,	1224	998	956	55	111
Oxford,	Worcester,	2380	3034	2713	218	214
Palmer,	Hampden,	3974	4082	3080	256	146
Paxton,	Worcester,	820	725	626	91	25
Peabody,	Essex, fr. Danvers	6549	6051	494	277
Pelham,	Hampshire,	983	748	737	39	55
Pembroke,	Plymouth,	1388	1524	1488	106	107
Pepperell,	Middlesex,	1754	1895	1709	180	103
Peru,	Berkshire,	519	499	494	75	17
Petersham,	Worcester,	1527	1465	1428	97	117
Phillipston,	"	809	764	725	73	43
Pittsfield,	Berkshire,	5872	8045	9676	435	835
Plainfield,	Hampshire,	814	639	579	94	
Plymouth,	Plymouth,	6024	6272	6068	593	356
Plympton,	"	927	994	924	112	71
Prescott,	Hampshire,	737	611	596	49	55
Princeton,	Worcester,	1318	1201	1239	162	39
Provincetown,	Barnstable,	3157	3206	3472	269	72
Quincy,	Norfolk,	5017	6778	6718	348	650
Randolph,	"	4741	5760	5734	386	564
Raynham,	Bristol,	1541	1746	1868	169	53
Reading,	Middlesex,	3108	2662	2436	375	123
Rehoboth,	Bristol,	2104	1932	1843	171	129
Richmond,	Berkshire,	907	914	944	42	68
Rochester,	Plymouth,	3808	1232	1156	163	34
Rockport,	Essex,	3274	3237	3367	371	110
Rowe,	Franklin,	659	619	563	43	5
Rowley,	Essex,	1075	1278	1191	86	134
Roxbury,†	Norfolk,	18364	25137	28426	1135	1986
Royalston,	Worcester,	1546	1486	1441	220	21
Russell,	Hampden,	521	605	618	38	45

* Portion annexed to Newburyport. † Annexed to Boston.

Town.	County.	1850	1860	1865	Butl'k.	Adams
Rutland,	Worcester,	1223	1076	1011	113	70
Salem,	Essex,	20264	22252	21189	1279	1013
Salisbury,	"	3100	3310	3609	331	274
Sandisfield,	Berkshire,	· 1649	1585	1411	87	44
Sandwich,	Barnstable,	4368	4479	4158	293	258
Saugus,	Essex,	1552	2024	2006	224	148
Savoy,	Berkshire,	955	904	866	59	41
Scituate,	Plymouth,	2149	2227	2269	215	195
Seekonk,	Bristol,	2243	2662	928	68	78
Sharon,	Norfolk,	1128	1377	1393	133	89
Sheffield,	Berkshire,	2769	2621	2459	162	184
Shelburne,	Franklin,	1239	1448	1564	177	19
Sherborn,	Middlesex,	1043	1129	1049	141	49
Shirley,	"	1158	1468	1217	120	81
Shrewsbury,	Worcester,	1596	1558	1570	204	83
Shutesbury,	Franklin,	912	798	788	79	42
Somerset,	Bristol,	1166	1793	1789	209	61
Somerville,	Middlesex,	3540	8025	9353	569	407
Southampton,	Hampshire,	1060	1130	1216	137	17
Southboro',	Worcester,	1347	1854	1750	202	106
Southbridge,	"	2824	3575	4131	240	130
South Danvers,	Essex,	Now Peabody, which see				
South Hadley,	Hampshire,	2495	2277	2099	237	60
South Reading,	Middlesex,	Now Wakefield, which see				
South Scituate,	Plymouth,	1770	1774	1635	205	93
Southwick,	Hampden,	1120	1188	1155	52	188
Spencer,	Worcester,	2244	2777	3024	253	59
Springfield,	Hampden,	11766	15199	22035	1699	1096
Sterling,	Worcester,	1805	1881	1668	193	102
Stockbridge,	Berkshire,	1941	2136	1967	162	121
Stoneham,	Middlesex,	2085	3206	3298	376	246
Stoughton,	Norfolk,	3494	4830	4855	427	305
Stow,	Middlesex,	1455	1641	1537	127	128
Sturbridge,	Worcester,	2119	2291	1993	171	52
Sudbury,	Middlesex,	1578	1691	1703	152	135
Sunderland,	Franklin,	792	839	861	137	1
Sutton,	Worcester,	2595	2676	2363	139	200
Swampscott,	Essex,	fr. Lynn	1530	1535	181	65
Swanzey,	Bristol,	1554	1430	1336	135	81
Taunton,	"	10441	15376	16005	1455	490
Templeton,	Worcester,	2173	2816	2390	334	139
Tewksbury,	Middlesex,	1044	1744	1801	96	70
Tisbury,	Dukes,	1803	1631	1698	111	25
Tolland,	Hampden,	594	596	511	34	36
Topsfield,	Essex,	1170	1292	1212	150	77
Townsend,	Middlesex,	1947	2005	2042	200	180
Truro,	Barnstable,	2051	1583	1447	37	13
Tyngsboro',	Middlesex,	799	626	578	45	61
Tyringham,	Berkshire,	821	730	650	40	55
Upton,	Worcester,	2023	1986	2018	272	90
Uxbridge,	"	2457	3133	2838	211	169
Wakefield,	Middlesex,	2407	3207	3244	433	218
Wales,	Hampden,	711	677	666	80	24

Town.	County.	1850	1860	1865	Bull'k.	Adams
Walpole,	Norfolk,	1929	2037	2018	194	133
Waltham,	Middlesex,	4464	6397	6896	558	451
Ware,	Hampshire,	3785	3597	3374	276	143
Wareham,	Plymouth,	3186	3186	2798	169	145
Warren,	Worcester,	1777	2107	2180	281	56
Warwick,	Franklin,	1021	932	901	87	75
Washington,	Berkshire,	953	948	859	42	41
Watertown,	Middlesex,	2837	3270	3779	297	158
Wayland,	"	1115	1188	1137	125	86
Webster,	Worcester,	2371	2912	3608	211	228
Wellfleet,	Barnstable,	2411	2322	2296	164	30
Wendell, ·	Franklin,	920	704	603	29	66
Wenham,	Essex,	977	1105	918	93	77
Westborough,	Worcester,	2371	2913	3141	343	165
West Boylston,	"	1749	2509	2294	259	91
W. Bridgew'r,	Plymouth,	1447	1846	1825	140	111
W. Brookfield,	Worcester,	1344	1548	1549	146	75
Westfield,	Hampden,	4180	5055	5634	343	617
Westford,	Middlesex,	1173	1624	1568	140	163
Westhampton,	Hampshire,	602	608	636	75	5
Westminster,	Worcester,	1914	1840	1639	244	68
W. Newbury,	Essex,	1746	2202	2087	193	184
Weston,	Middlesex,	1205	1243	1231	149	6
Westport,	Bristol,	2795	2767	2799	249	47
West Roxbury,	Norfolk, fr. Roxbury		6310	6912	431	410
W. Springfield,	Hampden,	2979	2105	2100	160	117
W.Stockbridge,	Berkshire,	1713	1589	1620	147	90
Weymouth,	Norfolk,	5369	7742	7975	757	695
Whately,	Franklin,	1101	1057	1012	81	91
Wilbraham,	Hampden,	2127	2081	2111	228	91
Williamsburg,	Hampshire,	1537	2095	1976	239	86
Williamstown,	Berkshire,	2626	2611	2555	262	155
Wilmington,	Middlesex,	874	919	850	82	68
Winchendon,	Worcester,	2445	2624	2801	418	118
Winchester,	Middlesex,	1353	1937	1968	235	130
Windsor,	Berkshire,	897	839	753	68	58
Winthrop,	Suffolk, fr. N. Chelsea		544	633	21	63
Woburn,	Middlesex,	3956	6287	6999	501	650
Worcester,	Worcester,	17049	24960	30055	2548	1857
Worthington,	Hampshire,	1134	1041	925	160	18
Wrentham,	Norfolk,	3037	3406	3072	313	111
Yarmouth,	Barnstable,	2505	2752	2472	175	44

IN 1861, most of the former town of Fall River, R. I., was annexed to Fall River, Mass., and a part of Portsmouth, R. I., annexed to Westport, Mass. The town lines between Seekonk and Pawtucket, then both in Mass., were adjusted, largely in favor of Pawtucket, which was transferred to Rhode Island. Massachusetts lost and Rhode Island gained about 2500 inhabitants by this settlement of boundaries.

RECAPITULATION BY COUNTIES.

Counties.	1840	1850	1860	1865	Bull'k.	Adams
Barnstable,	32548	35276	35990	34610	2230	997
Berkshire,	41745	45591	55120	56944	4137	3773
Bristol,	60164	76192	93794	89395	8407	3137
Dukes,	3958	4540	4403	4200	270	99
Essex,	94987	131300	165611	171034	13472	10803
Franklin,	28812	30870	31434	31340	3429	1392
Hampden,	37366	51283	57366	64570	4551	3906
Hampshire,	30897	35732	37823	39269	4353	1345
Middlesex,	106611	161383	216354	220384	17974	14345
Nantucket,	9012	8452	6094	4748	321	40
Norfolk,	53140	78892	109950	116306	8074	7862
Plymouth,	47373	55697	64768	63107	6442	3943
Suffolk,	95773	144517	192700	208212	8555	9908
Worcester,	95313	130789	159659	162912	16091	8810
	737,699	994,514	1,231,066	1,267,031	98,306	70,360
				Scattering,		125

VOTE OF MASSACHUSETTS SINCE 1854.

	Republican.		Democratic.	
1854, Gov.,	H. J. Gardner, Am.,	81,503	Henry W. Bishop.	13,642
	Emory Washb'rn, W.,	27,279	Henry Wilson, F. S.,	6,483
1855, "	Julius Rockwell,	36,521	Erasmus D. Beach,	34,920
	H. J. Gardner, Am.,	51,674	Sam'l H. Walley,W.,	14,454
1856, "	" " " A. Rep.,	92,467	Erasmus D. Beach,	40 082
	Josiah Quincy,	5,625	Luther V. Bell, W.,	7,075
			G. W. Gordon, Fill.,	10,385
1856, Pres.,	John C. Fremont,	108,515	James Buchanan,	39,287
			Mill'rd Fillmore, A.,	19,679
1857, Gov.,	Nathaniel P. Banks,	60,807	Erasmus D. Beach,	31,760
	H. J. Gardner, Am.,	37,596		
1858, "	Nathaniel P. Banks,	69,049	" " "	38,474
	A. A. Lawrence, A.,	12,084		
1859, "	Nathaniel P. Banks,	58,780	Benj. F. Butler,	35,334
	Geo. N. Briggs, Am.,	14,365		
1860, "	John A. Andrew,	104,527	E. D. Beach, Doug.,	35,191
	A. A. Lawrence, Bell,	23,816	B. F. Butler, Breck.,	6,000
1860, Pres.,	Abraham Lincoln,	106,533	Stephen A. Douglas,	34,372
	John Bell, Union,	22,331	J. C. Breckinridge,	5,939
1861, Gov.,	John A. Andrew,	65,261	Isaac Davis,	31,266
1862, "	" " "	80,835	Chas. Devens, Peo.,	52,587
1863, "	" " "	70,483	Henry W. Paine,	29,207
1864, "	" " "	125,281	" " "	49,190
1864, Pres.,	Abraham Lincoln,	126,742	Geo. B. McClellan,	48,745
1865, Gov.,	Alex'der H. Bullock,	69,912	Darius N. Couch,	21,245
1866, "	" " " "	92,012	Theo. H. Sweetser,	26,671
1867, "	" " " "	98,306	John Q. Adams,	70,360

VOTE FOR MEMBERS OF CONGRESS, 1866.

Republican.		Democratic.	
Dis. 1—Thomas D. Eliot,	8,184	Matthias Ellis,	1,539
2—Oakes Ames,	9,581	Abijah M. Ide,	2,456
3—Ginery Twichell,	6,084	William Aspinwall,	2,601
P. R. Guiney, Work.,	463		
4—Samuel Hooper,	7,902	Joseph M. Wightman,	3,183
5—Benjamin F. Butler,	9,021	William D. Northend,	2,838
6—Nathaniel P. Banks,	10,075	Frederick O. Prince,	3,366
7—George S. Boutwell,	9,847	Leverett Saltonstall,	2,885
8—John D. Baldwin,	9,039	William A. Williams,	1,901
9—William B. Washburn,	11,895	Levi Heywood,	1,768
10—Henry L. Dawes,	8,125	Chester W. Chapin,	4,185

INDUSTRY OF MASSACHUSETTS.

In looking over the volume of Industrial Statistics of Massachusetts, taken May 1st, 1865, we find an interesting Table which gives the statistics of the State for two periods of ten years interval, viz.: 1855 and 1865.

In 1855 the productions of 245,908 persons engaged in industrial pursuits were valued at $295,820,682, showing the average of each person to be $1202.97. This result was most satisfactory, but in 1865 the progress of the preceding ten years was shown by the official returns to be quite astonishing; for in the last year the statistics revealed the fact that the value of the productions of 271,421 persons was $517,240,613, or an average of $1905.67. This last, it should be borne in mind, was in a time of war, during the progress of which 159,000 of the men of Massachusetts had been engaged in the work of suppressing the rebellion, some for the whole four years and others for a shorter period. The leading and most valuable articles of manufactures or productions were the following: Cotton goods, $54,436,881; boots and shoes, $52,915,243; woolen goods, $48,430,671, calico and delaines, $25,258,703; clothing, $17,743,894; tanning and currying, $15,821,712; hay, $13,195,274; paper, $9,008,521, &c.

During the late rebellion Massachusetts contributed to the Federal Army and Navy, an aggregate of 159,165 men, and she expended for the war out of her own Treasury, $27,705,169, besides the expenditures of her cities and towns.

RHODE ISLAND.

Population in 1850 and 1860 by each United States census, and by the State census of 1865. Candidates for Governor in 1868: Ambrose E. Burnside, Republican; Lyman Pierce, Democrat.

Town.	County.	Population 1850	1860	1865	Governor '68. Burn.	Pierce
Barrington,	Bristol,	795	1000	1028	92	47
Bristol,	"	4616	5271	4649	312	99
Burrillville,	Providence,	3538	4140	4861	316	237
Charlestown,	Washington,	994	981	1134	94	74
Coventry,	Kent,	3620	4247	3395	212	67
Cranston,	Providence,	4310	7500	9177	161	326
Cumberland,	"	6661	8339	8216	240	117
E. Greenwich,	Kent,	2358	2882	2400	232	145
E. Providence,	Providence,	fr. Mass.		2172	70	186
Exeter,	Washington,	1634	1741	1498	73	38
Foster,	Providence,	1932	1935	1873	156	59
Glocester,	"	2872	2427	2286	85	190
Hopkinton,	Washington,	2477	2738	2512	213	22
Jamestown,	Newport,	358	400	349	46	36
Johnston,	Providence,	2937	3440	3436	63	119
Little Compton,	Newport,	1462	1304	1197	206	5
Middletown,	"	830	1012	1019	94	21
Newport,	"	9563	10508	12688	594	152
New Shoreham,	"	1262	1320	1308	84	79
No. Kingstown,	Washington,	2971	3104	3166	271	291
No. Providence,	Providence,	7680	11818	14553	719	617
Pawtucket,	"	3753	4200	5000	237	248
Portsmouth,	Newport,	1833	2048	2153	131	38
Providence,	Providence,	41513	50666	54595	2680	1137
Richmond,	Washington,	1784	1964	1830	156	130
Scituate,	Providence,	4582	4251	3538	234	126
Smithfield,	"	11500	13283	12315	602	191
So. Kingstown,	Washington,	3807	4717	4513	278	254
Tiverton,	Newport,	4699	1927	1973	68	37
Warren,	Bristol,	3103	2636	2792	227	195
Warwick,	Kent,	7740	8916	7696	381	190
Westerly,	Washington,	2763	3474	3815	270	37
W. Greenwich,	Kent,	1350	1258	1228	126	56
Woonsocket,	Providence,	fr. Cumberland,			331	143

In 1850 and 1860 most of Pawtucket and all of East Providence were in Massachusetts, while in 1861, the same year the transfer was made, the whole of Fall River and part of Tiverton were ceded to Massachusetts.

4

RECAPITULATION BY COUNTIES.

County	Population in 1840	1850	1860	1865	Governor, 1867. Burn.	Pierce
Bristol,	6476	8514	8907	8469	631	341
Kent,	13083	15068	17303	15319	951	458
Newport,	16874	20007	18519	20087	1223	368
Providence,	58073	87079	111999	122022	5884	3696
Washington,	14324	16430	18715	18468	1355	846
	108,830	147,098	175,443	184,965	10,044	5,709

VOTE OF RHODE ISLAND SINCE 1854.

	Republican.		Democratic.	
1854, Gov.,	William W. Hoppin,	9,112	Francis M. Dimond,	6,484
1855, " " " "		11,117	Americus V. Potter,	2,681
1856, " " " "		10,035	" " "	7,158
1856, Pres.,	John C. Fremont,	11,467	James Buchanan,	6,680
			Mill'd Fillmore, Am.,	1,675
1857, Gov.,	Elisha Dyer,	9,621	Americus V. Potter,	5,123
1858, " " "		7,934	Elisha R. Potter,	3,572
1859, "	Thomas G. Turner,	8,938	" " "	3,546
1860, "	Seth Padelford,	10,835	Wm. Sprague,Cons.,	12,295
1860, Pres.,	Abraham Lincoln,	12,244	Doug., Breck. & Bell,	7,707
1861, Gov.,	James Y. Smith,	10,200	Wm. Sprague,Cons.,	11,844
1862, "	William Sprague,	11,195	Scattering,	62
1863, "	James Y. Smith,	10,828	William C. Cozzens,	7,537
1864, " " " "		8,840	George H. Browne,	7,302
	A.C. Barstow, Ind. R.,	1,339		
1864, Pres.,	Abraham Lincoln,	14,349	Geo. B. McClellan,	8,718
1865, Gov.,	James Y. Smith,	10,061	Scattering,	753
1866, "	Ambrose E. Burnside,	8,197	Lyman Pierce,	2,816
1867, " " " "		7,372	" "	3,178
1868, " " " "		10,044	" "	5,709

VOTE FOR MEMBERS OF CONGRESS, 1867.

	Republican.		Democratic.	
Dis. 1—	Thomas A. Jenckes,	4,311	Scattering,	101
2—	Nathan F. Dixon,	2,669	Judge Carder,	1,480

RHODE ISLAND in 1860 ranked as the 33rd State in territorial extent, being the lowest, and was the 29th in population, yet as regards wealth she was among the highest, the average being nearly $800 to each person.

CONNECTICUT.

Population in 1850 and 1860 by each United States census. Candidates for Governor in 1868: Marshall Jewell, Republican; James E. English, Democrat.

Town.	County.	Population 1850	Population 1860	Governor '68. Jewell.	Governor '68. Eng.
Andover,	Tolland,	500	517	59	78
Ashford,	Windham,	1295	1231	151	162
Avon,	Hartford,	995	1059	129	92
Barkhamsted,	Litchfield,	1524	1272	176	166
Berlin,	Hartford,	1869	2146	292	230
Bethany,	New Haven,	914	974	80	161
Bethel,	Fairfield,		1711	228	168
Bethlem,	Litchfield,	815	815	74	95
Bloomfield,	Hartford,	1412	1401	102	215
Bolton,	Tolland,	600	683	48	85
Bozrah,	New London,	867	1216	107	69
Branford,	New Haven,	1423	2123	186	369
Bridgeport,	Fairfield,	7560	13299	1453	1638
Bridgewater,	Litchfield,		1048	45	187
Bristol,	Hartford,	2884	3436	392	445
Brookfield,	Fairfield,	1359	1224	113	165
Brooklyn,	Windham,	1514	2136	216	117
Burlington,	Hartford,	1161	1031	79	192
Canaan,	Litchfield,	2627	2834	91	194
Canterbury,	Windham,	1669	1591	167	188
Canton,	Hartford,	1986	2373	302	226
Chaplin,	Windham,	796	781	93	81
Chatham,	Middlesex,	1525	1766	203	194
Cheshire,	New Haven,	1626	2407	208	275
Chester,	Middlesex,	992	1015	140	104
Clinton,	"	1344	1427	215	135
Colchester,	New London,	2468	2862	285	250
Colebrook,	Litchfield,	1317	1375	150	143
Columbia,	Tolland,	876	832	77	116
Cornwall,	Litchfield,	2041	1953	176	222
Coventry,	Tolland,	1984	2085	263	138
Cromwell,	Middlesex,		1617	136	162
Danbury,	Fairfield,	5964	7234	836	785
Darien,	"	1454	1705	187	118
Derby,	New Haven,	3824	5443	660	663
Durham,	Middlesex,	1026	1130	134	130
Eastford,	Windham,	1127	1005	138	94
East Granby,	Hartford,		833	70	135
East Haddam,	Middlesex,	2610	3056	343	234
East Hartford,	Hartford,	2497	2951	355	326
East Haven,	New Haven,	1670	2292	312	270
East Lyme,	New London,	1382	1506	154	179
Easton,	Fairfield,	1432	1350	148	176

Town.	County.	1850	1860	Jewell.	Eng.
East Windsor,	Hartford,	2633	2580	278	233
Ellington,	Tolland,	1399	1510	175	160
Enfield,	Hartford,	4460	4997	430	330
Essex,	Middlesex,	950	1764	253	168
Fairfield,	Fairfield,	3614	4379	467	492
Farmington,	Hartford,	2630	3144	423	332
Franklin,	New London,	895	2358	79	93
Glastenbury,	Hartford,	3390	3363	356	367
Goshen,	Litchfield,	1457	1381	138	111
Granby,·	Hartford,	2498	1720	223	173
Greenwich,	Fairfield,	5036	6522	412	675
Griswold,	New London,	2065	2217	251	158
Groton,	" "	3743	4450	530´	430
Guilford,	New Haven,	2653	2624	333	276
Haddam,	Middlesex,	2279	2307	186	318
Hamden,	New Haven,	2164	2725	235	348
Hampton,	Windham,	946	936	120	78
Hartford,	Hartford,	13555	29152	2918	3574
Hartland,	"	848	846	68	104
Harwinton,	Litchfield,	1175	1044	152	93
Hebron,	Tolland,	1345	1425	177	128
Huntington,	Fairfield,	1301	1477	157	137
Kent,	Litchfield,	1848	1855	162	182
Killingly,	Windham,	4543	4926	579	423
Killingworth,	Middlesex,	1107	1126	87	169
Lebanon,	New London,	1961	2174	279	149
Ledyard,	" "	1558	1615	170	145
Lisbon,	" "	938	1262	53	71
Litchfield,	Litchfield,	3953	3200	286	354
Lyme,	New London,	2668	1246	150	130
Madison,	New Haven,	1837	1865	257	247
Manchester,	Hartford,	2546	3294	412	243
Mansfield,	Tolland,	2517	1697	294	196
Marlborough,	Hartford,	832	682	50	93
Meriden,	New Haven,	3559	7426	1134	882
Middlebury,	" "	763	664	93	51
Middlefield,	Middlesex,			116	72
Middletown,	"	8441	8610	786	955
Milford,	New Haven,	2465	2828	315	425
Monroe,	Fairfield,	1442	1382	124	177
Montville,	New London,	1848	2141	238	174
Morris,	Litchfield,		769	65	114
Naugatuck,	New Haven,	1720	2590	207	317
New Britain,	Hartford,	3029	5212	738	717
New Canaan,	Fairfield,	2600	2771	282	260
New Fairfield,	"	927	915	74	115
New Hartford,	Litchfield,	2643	2758	306	257
New Haven,	New Haven,	22533	39267	3524	5777
New London,	New London,	8991	10115	866	892
New Milford,	Litchfield,	4058	3535	352	421
Newtown,	Fairfield,	3338	3578	263	443
Norfolk,	Litchfield,	1643	1803	157	125
North Branford,	New Haven,	998	1050	141	105

Town.	County.	1850	1860	Jewell.	Eng.
North Canaan,	Litchfield,			106	193
North Haven,	New Haven,	1325	1499	197	160
North Stonington,	New London,	1936	1913	252	175
Norwalk,	Fairfield,	4651	7582	978	829
Norwich,	New London,	10265	14048	1558	1248
Old Lyme,	" "		1304	127	163
Old Saybrook,	Middlesex,		1105	139	112
Orange,	New Haven,	1476	1974	265	197
Oxford,	" "	1564	1269	141	190
Plainfield,	Windham,	2732	3665	338	298
Plymouth,	Litchfield,	2568	3244	468	308
Pomfret,	Windham,	1848	1673	189	104
Portland,	Middlesex,	2836	3657	263	208
Preston,	New London,	1842	2092	162	300
Prospect,	New Haven,	666	574	75	62
Putnam,	Windham,		2722	344	111
Redding,	Fairfield,	1754	1652	185	164
Ridgefield,	"	2237	2213	245	229
Rocky Hill,	Hartford,	1042	1102	88	120
Roxbury,	Litchfield,	1114	992	101	155
Salem,	New London,	764	830	92	93
Salisbury,	Litchfield,	3103	3100	227	416
Saybrook,	Middlesex,	2904	1213	185	106
Scotland,	Windham,		720	93	77
Seymour,	New Haven,	1677	1749	204	273
Sharon,	Litchfield,	2507	2556	196	330
Sherman,	Fairfield,	984	911	79	122
Simsbury,	Hartford,	2737	2410	182	198
Somers,	Tolland,	1598	1517	152	176
Southbury,	New Haven,	1484	1346	142	173
Southington,	Hartford,	2135	3315	404	454
South Windsor,	"	1638	1789	173	222
Sprague,	New London,			103	180
Stafford,	Tolland,	2540	3397	389	388
Stamford,	Fairfield,	5000	7185	686	673
Sterling,	Windham,	1025	1051	117	105
Stonington,	New London,	5431	5827	559	482
Stratford,	Fairfield,	2040	2294	273	261
Suffield,	Hartford,	2962	3230	379	358
Thompson,	Windham,	4638	3259	401	158
Tolland,	Tolland,	1406	1310	133	182
Torrington,	Litchfield,	1916	2278	359	247
Trumbull,	Fairfield,	1309	1474	141	187
Union,	Tolland,	728	732	94	83
Vernon,	"	2900	3838	594	283
Voluntown,	Windham,	1064	1055	155	100
Wallingford,	New Haven,	2595	3206	304	395
Warren,	Litchfield,	830	710	66	91
Washington,	"	1802	1659	163	199
Waterbury,	New Haven,	5137	10004	916	1243
Waterford,	New London,	2259	2555	215	248
Watertown,	Litchfield,	1533	1587	237	137
Westbrook,	Middlesex,	1202	1056	146	101

Town.	County.	1850	1860	1865	Jewell.	Eng.
West Hartford,	Hartford,	4411	1296	186	141	
Weston,	Fairfield,	1056	1117	56	159	
Westport,	"	2651	3293	226	336	
Wethersfield,	Hartford,	2523	2705	265	200	
Willington,	Tolland,	1388	1166	156	107	
Wilton,	Fairfield,	2006	2208	209	197	
Winchester,	Litchfield,	2179	3515	459	327	
Windham,	Windham,	4503	4711	477	287	
Windsor,	Hartford,	3294	2280	236	291	
Windsor Locks,	"		1587	127	206	
Wolcott,	New Haven,	603	574	45	64	
Woodbridge,	" "	912	872	115	60	
Woodbury,	Litchfield,	2150	2037	266	216	
Woodstock,	Windham,	3381	3285	451	157	

RECAPITULATION BY COUNTIES.

County.	Population in 1840	1850	1860	Governor, 1868. Jewell.	Eng.
Fairfield,	49917	59775	77476	7831	8596
Hartford,	55629	69967	89962	9657	10217
Litchfield,	40448	45253	47318	4978	5283
Middlesex,	24879	27216	30857	3352	3168
New Haven,	48619	65588	97345	10089	12983
New London,	44463	51821	61731	6230	5629
Tolland,	17980	20091	20709	2611	2125
Windham,	28080	31081	34747	4029	2540
	309,978	370,792	460,147	48,777	50,541
				Scattering,	7

VOTE FOR MEMBERS OF CONGRESS, 1867.

Republican.		Democratic.	
Dis. 1—Henry C. Deming,	11,477	Richard D. Hubbard,	11,994
2—Cyrus Northrop,	12,937	Julius Hotchkiss,	14,730
3—H. H. Starkweather,	9,723	Earl Martin,	7,827
4—Phineas T. Barnum,	12,103	William H. Barnum,	13,083

By the census of 1860, Connecticut was shown to be the richest State in the Union in proportion to the number of her inhabitants, the total valuation having been $444,274,114, over $950 to each person. The State debt is $7,324,000; it was reduced $337,000 the last year.

VOTE OF CONNECTICUT SINCE 1854.

	Republican.		Democratic.	
1854, Gov.,	Henry Dutton,	19,465	Samuel Ingham,	28,538
	Chas. Chapman, W.,	10,672		
1855, "	Henry Dutton,	9,162	" "	27,290
	Wm. T. Minor, Am.,	28,028		
1856, "	" " " .	26,108	" "	32,704
	Gideon Welles,	6,740		
1856, Pres.,	John C. Fremont,	42,715	James Buchanan,	34,995
			Mill'd Fillmore, Am.,	2,615
1857, Gov.,	Alexand'r H. Holley,	31,702	Samuel Ingham,	31,156
1858, "	Wm. A. Buckingham,	36,298	James T. Pratt,	33,545
1859, "	" " "	40,239	" " "	38,369
1830, "	" " "	44,458	Thos. H. Seymour,	43,917
1860, Pres.,	Abraham Lincoln,	43,792	Stephen A. Douglas,	15,522
	John Bell, Union,	3,291	J. C. Breckinridge,	14,641
1861, Gov.,	Wm. A. Buckingham,	43,012	James C. Loomis,	40,926
1862, "	" " "	39,782	" " "	30,634
1863, "	" " "	41,032	Thos. H. Seymour,	38,395
1864, "	" " "	39,820	Origen S. Seymour,	34,162
1864, Pres.,	Abraham Lincoln,	44,691	Geo. B. McClellan,	42,285
1865, Gov.,	Wm. A. Buckingham,	42,374	Origen S. Seymour,	31,339
1866, "	Joseph R. Hawley,	43,974	James E. English,	43,433
1867, "	" " " "	46,578	" " "	47,565
1868, "	Marshall Jewell,	48,777	" " "	50,541

VITAL STATISTICS OF CONNECTICUT. An official report shows that during the year 1867 there were 12,029 births in Connecticut, which is the largest number ever reported in any one year in the State, and is an increase of 406 over the number returned for 1866. The excess of births over deaths was 4,686. There were 4,779 marriages in 1867, which was the greatest number ever reported in any one year except 1866. Two-thirds of the marriages were between native Americans; two were between blacks and whites. During the year 7,343 deaths were registered, which is 177 less than in 1866. The leading disease was consumption, from which there have been 14,951 deaths during the past fourteen years. During the year 459 divorces were granted, which is 29 less than in 1866. More than two-thirds were granted upon the petitions of wives.

SINCE 1821 Connecticut has voted for President as follows: J. Q. Adams, twice; Henry Clay, twice; Martin Van Buren, W. H. Harrison, Zachary Taylor, Franklin Pierce and J. C. Fremont, once each; Abraham Lincoln twice. The Democrats have been twice successful; their opponents nine times.

POPULAR VOTE FOR PRESIDENT.

States.	1860.				1864.	
	Lincoln.	Douglas.	Breck.	Bell.	Lincoln.	McClell.
Alabama,		13,651	48,831	27,875	No vote.	
Arkansas,		5,227	28,732	20,094	"	"
California,	39,173	38,516	34,334	6,817	62,134	43,841
Connecticut,	43,792	15,522	14,641	3,291	44,691	42,285
Delaware,	3,815	1,023	7,337	3,864	8,155	8,767
Florida,		367	8,543	5,437	No vote.	
Georgia,		11,590	51,889	42,886	"	"
Illinois,	172,161	160,215	2,404	4,913	189,496	158,730
Indiana,	139,033	115,509	12,295	5,306	150,422	130,233
Iowa,	70,409	55,111	1,048	1,763	89,075	49,595
Kansas,	Admitted in 1861.				16,441	3,691
Kentucky,	1,364	25,651	53,143	66,058	27,786	64,304
Louisiana,		7,625	22,681	20,204	No vote.	
Maine,	62,811	26,693	6,368	2,046	68,144	46,992
Maryland,	2,294	5,966	42,482	41,760	40,153	32,739
Massachusetts,	106,533	34,372	5,939	22,331	126,742	48,745
Michigan,	88,480	65,057	805	405	91,521	74,604
Minnesota,	22,069	11,920	748	62	25,060	17,375
Mississippi.		3,283	40,797	25,040	No vote.	
Missouri,	17,028	58,801	31,317	58,372	72,750	31,678
Nebraska.	Admitted in 1866.					
Nevada,	"	" 1864.			9,826	6,564
N. Hampshire,	37,519	25,881	2,112	441	36,400	32,871
New Jersey,	58,324	62,801 Coalition.			60,723	68,024
New York,	362,646	312,510	"		368,735	361,986
No. Carolina,		2,701	48,539	44,950	No vote.	
Ohio,	231,610	187,232	11,405	12,194	265,154	205,568
Oregon,	5,270	3,951	5,006	183	9,888	8,457
Pennsylvania,	268,030	16,765	178,881	12,776	296,391	276,316
Rhode Island,	12,244	7,707 Coalition.			14,349	8,718
So. Carolina,	Legislature chose Electors.				No vote.	
Tennessee,		11,350	64,709	69,274	"	"
Texas,			47,548	15,438		
Vermont,	33,808	6,849	218	1,969	42,419	13,321
Virginia.	1,929	16,290	74,323	74,681	No vote.	
W. Virginia,	Admitted in 1862.				23,152	10,438
Wisconsin,	86,810	65,021	888	161	83,458	65,884
	1,866,452	1,375,157	847,953	590,631	2,223,035	1,811,754

ELECTORAL VOTES FOR PRESIDENT AND VICE PRESIDENT.

	President.		Vice President.	
1860	Abraham Lincoln,	180	Hannibal Hamlin,	180
	J. C. Breckinridge,	72	Joseph Lane,	72
	John Bell,	39	Edward Everett.	39
	Stephen A. Douglas,	12	Herschel V. Johnson,	12
1864	Abraham Lincoln,	213	Andrew Johnson,	213
	George B. McClellan,	21	George H. Pendleton,	21

ELECTORS, POPULAR VOTE AT LATEST ELECTION, &c.

States.	Electors 1868.	Time.	Repub.	Dem.	R. maj.	D. maj.	State election.
Ala.	8	1868	69,807	1,005	68,802		
Ark.	5	1868	27,913	26,597	1,316		
Cal.	5	1867	*a*40,359	49,905		9,546	1 Wed. Sept.
Ct.	6	1868	48,777	50,541		1,764	1 Mon. April.
Del.	3	1866	8,598	9,810		1,212	1 Tues. Nov.
Fla.	3	1868	*b*14,170	7,852	6,318		
Ga.	9	1868	83,237	76,008	7,229		
Ill.	16	1866	203,045	147,058	55,987		1 Tues. Nov.
Ind.	13	1866	169,601	155,399	14,202		2 Tues. Oct.
Iowa,	8	1867	89,749	62,950	26,799		2 Tues. Oct.
Kan.	3	1866	19,370	8,151	11,219		1 Tues. Nov.
Ky.	11	1867	*c*33,939	90,255		56,316	1 Mon. Aug.
La.	7	1868	64,961	*d*38,046	26,855		1 Tues. Nov.
Me.	7	1867	57,332	45,990	11,342		2 Mon. Sept.
Md.	7	1867	21,890	63,602		41,712	1 Tues. Nov.
Mass.	12	1867	98,306	70,360	27,946		1 Tues. Nov.
Mich.	8	1867	80,819	55,865	24,954		1 Tues. Nov.
Minn.	4	1867	34,870	29,543	5,327		1 Tues. Nov.
Miss.	7	1868	Reported Dem. maj. 11,630				
Mo.	11	1866	62,187	40,958	21,229		1 Tues. Nov.
Neb.	3	1866	4,820	4,072	748		1 Tues. Nov.
Nev.	3	1866	5,126	4,036	1,090		1 Tues. Nov.
N. H.	5	1868	39,724	37,098	2,626		2 Tues. March.
N. J.	7	1867	51,114	67,468		16,354	1 Tues. Nov.
N. Y.	33	1867	325,099	373,029		47,930	1 Tues. Nov.
N. C.	9	1868	92,590	71,820	20,770		
Ohio,	21	1867	243,605	240,622	2,983		2 Tues. Oct.
Ore.	3	1868	Reported Dem. maj. 1,200				1 Mon. June.
Pa.	26	1867	266,824	267,746		922	2 Tues. Oct.
R. I.	4	1868	10,044	5,709	4,335		1 Wed. April.
S. C.	6	1868	70,758	27,288	43,470		
Tenn.	10	1867	74,484	22,548	51,946		1 Tues. Nov.
Tex.	6		No recent election.				
Vt.	5	1867	31,694	11,510	20,184		1 Tues. Sept.
Va.	10		No recent election.				
W. Va.	5	1866	23,802	17,158	6,644		4 Thurs. Oct.
Wis.	8	1867	73,637	68,873	4,764		1 Tues. Nov.

317

a 2088 more for an Independent Republican; *b* 2292 more for an Independent; *c* 13,167 for a Union Democrat; *d* 3568 for the other Democratic candidates.

The elections to take place before the Presidential election, Nov. 3rd, are as follows: Kentucky, Aug. 3rd; Vermont, Sept. 1st; Maine, Sept. 11th; California on Presidential year votes on the day of that election; Indiana, Iowa, Ohio and Pennsylvania, Oct. 13th; West Virginia, Oct. 22nd.

AREA AND POPULATION BY STATES.

States.	Sq. Miles.	Total Population. 1850	1860	Classes in 1860. Whites.	Free Col.	Slaves
Alabama,	50,722	771,623	964,201	526,271	2,690	*435,080
Arkansas,	52,198	209,897	435,450	324,143	144	111,115
California,	188,982	92,597	379,994	358,110	4,086	
Connecticut,	4,674	370,792	460,147	451,504	8,627	
Delaware,	2,120	91,532	112,216	90,589	19,829	1,798
Florida,	59,268	87,445	140,424	77,747	932	61,745
Georgia,	58,000	906,185	1,057,286	591,550	3,500	462,198
Illinois,	55,409	851,470	1,711,951	1,704,291	7,628	
Indiana,	33,809	988,416	1,350,428	1,338,710	11,428	
Iowa,	50,914	192,214	674,913	673,779	1,069	
Kansas,	81,318		107,206	106,390	625	2
Kentucky,	37,680	982,405	1,155,684	919,484	10,684	225,483
Louisiana,	46,431	517,762	708,002	357,456	18,647	331,726
Maine,	31,766	583,169	628,279	626,947	1,327	
Maryland,	9,356	583,034	687,049	515,918	83,942	87,189
Massachus'ts,	7,800	994,514	1,231,066	1,221,432	9,602	
Michigan,	58,243	397,654	749,113	736,142	6,799	
Minnesota,	83,531	6,077	172,023	169,395	259	
Mississippi,	47,156	606,526	791,305	353,899	773	436,631
Missouri,	67,380	682,044	1,182,012	1,063,489	3,572	114,931
Nebraska,	75,995		28,841	28,696	67	15
Nevada,	81,539		6,857	6,812	45	
N. Hampshire,	9,280	317,976	326,073	325,579	494	
New Jersey,	8,320	489,555	672,035	646,699	25,318	†18
New York,	47,000	3,097,394	3,880,735	3,831,590	49,005	
N. Carolina,	50,704	869,039	992,622	629,942	30,463	331,059
Ohio,	39,964	1,980,329	2,339,511	2,302,808	36,673	
Oregon,	95,274	13,294	52,465	52,160	128	
Pennsylv'a,	46,000	2,311,786	2,906,215	2,849,259	56,949	
Rhode Island,	1,306	147,545	174,620	170,649	3,952	
So. Carolina,	29,385	668,507	703,708	291,300	9,914	402,406
Tennessee,	45,600	1,002,717	1,109,801	826,722	7,300	275,719
Texas,	237,321	212,592	604,215	420,891	355	182,566
Vermont,	10,212	314,120	315,098	314,369	709	
Virginia,	38,440		1,219,626	691,867	55,269	472,494
W. Virginia,	22,912	} 1,421,661 {	376,692	355,544	2,773	18,371
Wisconsin,	53,924	305,391	775,881	773,693	1,171	
Territories.						
Colorado,	105,818		34,277	34,231	46	
Dakota,	318,128		4,837	2,576		
D. Columbia,	60	51,687	75,080	60,763	11,131	3,185
N. Mexico,	243,063	61,547	93,516	82,924	85	
Utah,	128,835	11,380	40,273	40,125	30	29
Washington,	175,141		11,594	11,138	30	
		23,191,876	31,443,321	26,957,471	488,070	3,953,760

* The deficiency between white, free colored, slaves and total is made up by civilized Indians.   † Colored apprentices.

GOVERNORS OF STATES, ETC.

Republicans in Roman; Democrats in *Italic*.

States.	Governors.	Suc-ces'r El'd.	Com-plex Leg.	Next Legis. chosen.	Meets
Alabama,	William H. Smith,			1870	
Arkansas,	Powell Clayton,	1872	Rep	1870	1 Mon Nov
California,	*Henry H. Haight,*	1871	Dem	1868	1 Mon Dec
Connecticut,	*James E. English,*	1869	Rep	1869	1 Wed May
Delaware,	*Gove Saulsbury,*	1870	Dem	1868	1 Tues Jan
Florida,	Harrison Reed,	1872	Rep	1870	1 Mon Nov
Georgia,	Rufus B. Bullock,	1872	Rep	1870	1 Thurs Nov
Illinois,	Richard J. Oglesby,	1868	Rep	1868	2 Mon Jan
Indiana,	Conrad Baker,	1868	Rep	1868	1 Wed Jan
Iowa,	Samuel Merrill,	1869	Rep	1869	2 Mon Jan
Kansas,	Samuel J. Crawford,	1868	Rep	1868	2 Thurs Jan
Kentucky,	*John W. Stevenson,*	1868	Dem	1869	1 Mon Dec
Louisiana,	Henry C. Warmouth,	1872	Rep	1870	
Maine,	J. L. Chamberlain,	1868	Rep	1868	1 Wed Jan
Maryland,	*Odin Bowie,*	1871	Dem	1869	1 Wed Jan
Massachus'ts,	Alex. H. Bullock,	1868	Rep	1868	1 Wed Jan
Michigan,	Henry H. Crapo,	1868	Rep	1868	1 Wed Jan
Minnesota,	Wm. R. Marshall,	1869	Rep	1868	1 Tues Jan
Mississippi,	*Benj. J. Humphrey,*	1872	Dem	1870	1 Mon Jan
Missouri,	Thos. C. Fletcher,	1868	Rep	1868	4 Mon Dec
Nebraska,	David Butler,	1868	Rep	1868	
Nevada,	Henry G. Blasdell,	1868	Rep	1868	1 Mon Jan
N.Hampshire,	Walter Harriman,	1869	Rep	1869	1 Wed June
New Jersey,	*Marcus L. Ward,*	1868	Dem	1868	2 Tues Jan
New York,	Reuben E. Fenton,	1868	Dem	1868	1 Tues Jan
No. Carolina,	William W. Holden,	1870	Rep	1870	
Ohio,	Rutherford B. Hayes,	1869	Dem	1869	1 Mon Jan
Oregon,	*George L. Woods,*	1870	Dem	1870	2 Mon Sept
Pennsylv'a,	John W. Geary,	1869	Rep	1868	1 Tues Jan
Rhode Island,	Amb'se E. Burnside,	1869	Rep	1869	4 Wed May
So. Carolina,	Richard K. Scott,	1870	Rep	1870	
Tennessee,	Wm. G. Brownlow,	1869	Rep	1869	1 Mon Oct
Texas,	Edward M. Pease,	1868		1868	
Vermont,	John B. Page,	1868	Rep	1868	2 Thurs Oct
Virginia,	Henry H. Wells,	1868		1870	
W. Virginia,	Arthur I. Boreman,	1868	Rep	1868	3 Tues Jan
Wisconsin,	Lucius Fairchild,	1869	Rep	1868	2 Wed Jan

GOVERNORS OF TERRITORIES.

Alaska, —— Rousseau,
Arizona, R. C. McCormick.
Colorado, A. C. Hunt.
Dakota, Andrew J. Faulk.
Idaho, D. W. Ballard.

Montana, Greene C. Smith.
New Mexico, R. B. Mitchell.
Utah, Charles Durkee.
Washington, Wm. Pickering.

Governors of Territories are appointed by the President and Senate.

UNITED STATES GOVERNMENT.

July 15, 1868.

President, ANDREW JOHNSON, Tennessee.
Secretary of State, WILLIAM H. SEWARD, New York.
Secretary of Treasury, HUGH McCULLOCH, Indiana.
Secretary of War, JOHN M. SCHOFIELD, ———
Secretary of the Navy, GIDEON WELLES, Connecticut.
Secretary of the Interior, O. H. BROWNING, Illinois.
Postmaster-General, ALEX. W. RANDALL, Wisconsin.
Attorney-General, WILLIAM M EVARTS, New York.

SUPREME COURT.

SALMON P. CHASE, Ohio, *Chief Justice.*
NATHAN CLIFFORD, Maine, *Associate Justice.*
SAMUEL NELSON, New York,   "   "
ROBERT C. GRIER, Penn.,   "   "
DAVID DAVIS, Illinois,   "   "
NOAH H. SWAYNE, Ohio,   "   "
SAMUEL F. MILLER, Iowa,   "   "
STEPHEN J. FIELD, California, "   "

PRESIDENTS OF THE UNITED STATES.

George Washington,	1789 to 1797	John Tyler,	1841 to 1845
John Adams,	1797 to 1801	James K. Polk,	1845 to 1849
Thomas Jefferson,	1801 to 1809	Zachary Taylor,	1849 to 1850
James Madison,	1809 to 1817	Died in office.	
James Monroe,	1817 to 1825	Millard Fillmore,	1850 to 1853
John Q. Adams,	1825 to 1829	Franklin Pierce,	1853 to 1857
Andrew Jackson,	1829 to 1837	James Buchanan,	1857 to 1861
Martin Van Buren,	1837 to 1841	Abraham Lincoln,	1861 to 1865
Wm. H. Harrison,	1841 to 1841	Died in office.	
Died in office.		Andrew Johnson,	1865 to ——

FORTIETH CONGRESS, 1867–1869.

SENATE.

President pro tempore, BENJAMIN F. WADE, Ohio.

Secretary, GEORGE C. GORHAM, California.

States marked with an asterisk (*) not admitted to representation.
Names marked with an dagger (†) are Democrats.

	Term ex.		Term ex.
ALABAMA.		**MARYLAND.**	
ARKANSAS.		William P. Whyte,†	1869
Alexander McDonald,	1871	George Vickers,†	1873
Benjamin F. Rice,	1873	**MASSACHUSETTS.**	
CALIFORNIA.		Charles Sumner,	1869
John Conness,	1869	Henry Wilson,	1871
Cornelius Cole,	1873	**MICHIGAN.**	
CONNECTICUT.		Zachariah Chandler,	1869
James Dixon,†	1869	Jacob M. Howard,	1871
Orris S. Ferry,	1873	**MINNESOTA.**	
DELAWARE.		Alexander Ramsey,	1869
Willard Saulsbury,†	1871	Daniel S. Norton,†	1871
James A. Bayard,†	1873	**MISSISSIPPI.***	
FLORIDA.		**MISSOURI.**	
A. S. Welch,	1869	John B. Henderson,	1869
Thomas W. Osborne,	1873	Charles D. Drake,	1873
GEORGIA.		**NEBRASKA.**	
ILLINOIS.		Thomas W. Tipton.	1869
Richard Yates,	1871	John M. Thayer,	1871
Lyman Trumbull,	1873	**NEVADA.**	
INDIANA.		William M. Stewart,	1869
Thomas A. Hendricks,†	1869	James W. Nye,	1873
Oliver P. Morton,	1871	**NEW HAMPSHIRE.**	
IOWA.		Aaron H. Cragin,	1871
James W. Grimes,	1871	James W. Patterson,	1873
James Harlan,	1873	**NEW JERSEY.**	
KANSAS.		Fred'k T. Frelinghuysen,	1869
Edmund G. Ross,	1871	Alexander G. Cattell,	1871
Samuel C. Pomeroy,	1873	**NEW YORK.**	
KENTUCKY.		Edwin D. Morgan,	1869
Thomas C. McCreery,†	1871	Roscoe Conkling,	1873
Garrett Davis,†	1873	**NORTH CAROLINA.**	
LOUISIANA.		Joseph C. Abbott,	1871
John S. Harris,	1871	John Pool,	1873
William P. Kellogg,	1873	**OHIO.**	
MAINE.		Benjamin F. Wade,	1869
Lot M. Morrill,	1869	John Sherman,	1873
William P. Fessenden,	1871		

	Term ex.		Term ex.
OREGON.		**TENNESSEE.**	
George H. Williams,	1871	David T. Patterson,†	1869
Henry W. Corbett,	1873	Joseph S. Fowler,	1871
PENNSYLVANIA.		**VERMONT.**	
Charles R. Buckalew,†	1869	George F. Edmunds,	1869
Simon Cameron,	1873	Justin S. Morrill,	1873
RHODE ISLAND.		**VIRGINIA.***	
William Sprague,	1869	**WEST VIRGINIA.**	
Henry B. Anthony,	1871	Peter G Van Winkle,	1869
SOUTH CAROLINA.		Waitman T. Willey,	1871
Thomas J. Robertson,	1871	**WISCONSIN.**	
Frederick A. Sawyer,	1873	James R. Doolittle,†	1869
TEXAS.*		Timothy O. Howe,	1873

ELECTED TO SUCCEED THOSE WHOSE TERMS EXPIRE IN 1869.

California, Eugene Casserly.†   *Ohio*, Allen G. Thurman.†
Conn., William A. Buckingham.   *R I.*, William Sprague.
Florida, Abijah Gilbert.   *Tenn.*, Wm. G. Brownlow.
Maryland,William T. Hamilton.†

HOUSE OF REPRESENTATIVES.

Speaker, SCHUYLER COLFAX, Indiana.

Clerk, EDWARD McPHERSON, Pennsylvania.

States marked with an asterisk (*) not yet admitted to representation. Names marked with a dagger (†) are Democrats. The majority of each member at his election is given when known.

Dis.		Maj.	Dis.		Maj.
	ALABAMA.			**CONNECTICUT.**	
1	Francis W. Kellogg,		1	Richard D. Hubbard,†	517
2	Charles W. Buckley,		2	Julius Hotchkiss,†	1793
3	Benjamin W. Norris,		3	Henry H. Starkweather,	1896
4	Charles W. Pierce,		4	William H. Barnum,†	980
5	Joseph W. Burke,			**DELAWARE.**	
6	Thomas Haughey,		1	John A. Nicholson,†	1380
	ARKANSAS.			**GEORGIA.**	
1	Logan H. Roots,		1	J. W. Clift,	3810
2	James Hinds,		2	Nelson Tift,†	1502
3	Thomas Boles,		3	William P. Edwards,	925
	CALIFORNIA.		4	Samuel F. Gove,	2161
1	Samuel B. Axtell,†	4805	5	Charles H. Prince,	1772
2	William Higby,	1257	6	John H. Christy,†	1634
3	James A. Johnson,†	373	7	P. M. B. Young,†	3195

Dis.		Maj.
	FLORIDA.	
1	Charles M. Hamilton,	
	ILLINOIS.	
1	Norman B. Judd,	9580
2	John F. Farnsworth,	12839
3	Elihu B. Washburne,	8760
4	Abner C. Harding,	2561
5	Ebon C. Ingersoll,	8772
6	Burton C. Cook,	7294
7	Henry P. H. Bromwell,	4138
8	Shelby M. Cullom,	4103
9	Lewis W. Ross,†	775
10	Albert G. Burr,†	2373
11	Samuel S. Marshall,†	2290
12	Jehu Baker,	1076
13	Green B. Raum,	569
At large—John A. Logan,		55987
	INDIANA.	
1	William E. Niblack,†	1350
2	Michael C. Kerr,†	1743
3	Morton C. Hunter,	690
4	William S. Holman,†	869
5	George W. Julian,	6228
6	John Coburn,	2474
7	Henry D. Washburn,	513
8	Godlove S. Orth,	205
9	Schuyler Colfax,	2148
10	William Williams,	1272
11	John P. C. Shanks,	2877
	IOWA.	
1	James F. Wilson,	5891
2	Hiram Price,	7037
3	William B. Allison,	5002
4	William Loughridge,	6080
5	Granville M. Dodge,	4398
6	Asahel W. Hubbard,	6072
	KANSAS.	
1	Sidney Clarke,	11,196
	KENTUCKY.	
1	Lawrence S. Trimble,†	8007
2	Vacant, Dem.	6106
3	Jacob S. Golladay,†	5444
4	J. Proctor Knott,†	5922
5	Asa P. Grover,†	4701
6	Thomas L. Jones,†	5649
7	James B. Beck,†	8052
8	George M. Adams,†	515
9	Samuel McKee, Dem.	1479
	LOUISIANA.	
1	J. Hale Sypher,	
2	James Mann,†	
3	J. P. Newsham,	
4	Michel Vidal,	
5	William J. Blackburn.	

Dis.		Maj.
	MAINE.	
1	John Lynch,	3958
2	Sidney Perham,	6421
3	James G. Blaine,	6591
4	John A. Peters,	5495
5	Frederick A. Pike,	4378
	MARYLAND.	
1	Hiram McCullough,†	7677
2	Stevenson Archer,†	2077
3	Charles E. Phelps,†	980
4	Francis Thomas,	2022
5	Frederick Stone,†	6676
	MASSACHUSETTS.	
1	Thomas D. Eliot,	6645
2	Oakes Ames,	7125
3	Ginery Twichell,	3483
4	Samuel Hooper,	4719
5	Benjamin F. Butler,	6183
6	Nathaniel P. Banks,	6709
7	George S. Boutwell,	6962
8	John D. Baldwin,	7138
9	William B. Washburn,	10127
10	Henry L. Dawes,	3940
	MICHIGAN.	
1	Fernando C. Beaman,	3876
2	Charles Upson,	8395
3	Austin Blair,	3952
4	Thomas W. Ferry,	7152
5	Rowl'nd E. Trowbridge,	2382
6	John F. Driggs,	4039
	MINNESOTA.	
1	William Windom,	5940
2	Ignatius Donnelly,	4268
	MISSISSIPPI.*	
	MISSOURI.	
1	William A. Pile,	218
2	Carman A. Newcomb,	3310
3	James R. McCormick,†	190
4	Joseph J. Gravelly,	4154
5	Joseph W. McClurg,	3533
6	Robert T. Van Horn,	534
7	Benjamin F. Loan,	6962
8	John F. Benjamin,	1532
9	George W. Anderson,	178
	NEBRASKA.	
1	John Taffe,	748
	NEVADA.	
1	Delos R. Ashley,	852
	NEW HAMPSHIRE.	
1	Jacob H. Ela,	996
2	Aaron F. Stevens,	955
3	Jacob Benton,	1018
	OREGON.	
1	Rufus Mallory,	553

Dis.		Maj.	Dis.		Maj.
	NEW JERSEY.		4	William Lawrence,	2254
1	William Moore,	3360	5	William Mungen,†	2652
2	Charles Haight,†	349	6	Reader W. Clarke,	1579
3	Charles Sitgreaves,†	2813	7	Samuel Shellabarger,	2171
4	John Hill,	462	8	John Beatty,	835
5	George A. Halsey,	933	9	Ralph P. Buckland,	1287
	NEW YORK.		10	James M. Ashley,	1917
1	Stephen Taber,†	1096	11	John T. Wilson,	2838
2	Demas Barnes,†	6629	12	PhiladelphVan Trump,†	3210
3	William E. Robinson,†	1831	13	Columb. Delano,a Dem.	271
4	John Fox,†	10260	14	Martin Welker,	1707
5	John Morrisey,†	2659	15	Tobias A. Plants,	2064
6	Thomas E. Stewart,†	2497	16	John A. Bingham,	1422
7	John W. Chanler,†	4760	17	Ephraim R. Eckley,	4642
8	James Brooks,†	5606	18	Rufus P. Spalding,	6505
9	Fernando Wood,†	1610	19	James A. Garfield,	10986
10	William H. Robertson,	2055		**PENNSYLVANIA.**	
11	Charles H. Van Wyck,	261	1	Samuel J. Randall,†	4464
12	John H. Ketcham,	1695	2	Charles O'Neill,	3137
13	Thomas Cornell,	342	3	Leonard Myers,	1004
14	John V. L. Pruyn,†	648	4	William D. Kelley,	2425
15	John A. Griswold,	5316	5	Caleb N. Taylor,	459
16	Orange Ferris,	1929	6	Benjamin M. Boyer,†	2592
17	Calvin T. Hulburd,	8333	7	John M. Broomall,	3480
18	James M. Marvin,	3154	8	J. Lawrence Getz,†	6189
19	William C. Fields,	3656	9	Thaddeus Stevens,	5823
20	Addison H. Laflin,	4764	10	Henry L. Cake,	215
21	Alexander H. Bailey,	667	11	David M. Van Auken,†	6786
22	John C. Churchill,	5634	12	George W. Woodward,†	515
23	Dennis McCarthy,	5294	13	Ulysses Mercur,	1287
24	Theodore M. Pomeroy,	4785	14	George F. Miller,	1515
25	William H. Kelsey,	4303	15	Adam J. Glossbrenner,†	3341
26	William S. Lincoln,	5416	16	William H. Koontz,	625
27	Hamilton Ward,	6315	17	Daniel J. Morrell,	1319
28	Lewis Selye,	2034	18	Stephen F. Wilson,	2046
29	Burt Van Horn,	3073	19	Glenni W. Scofield,	2626
30	James M. Humphrey,†	1317	20	Darwin A. Finney,	1884
31	Henry Van Aernam,	7106	21	John Covode,	354
	NORTH CAROLINA.		22	James K. Moorhead,	3065
1	John R. French,		23	Thomas Williams,	4185
2	David Heaton,		24	George V. Lawrence,	1538
3	Oliver H. Dockery,			**RHODE ISLAND.**	
4	John T. Deweese,		1	Thomas A. Jenckes,	4210
5	Israel G. Lash,		2	Nathan F. Dixon,	1189
6	Nathaniel Boyden,†			**TEXAS.***	
7	Alexander H. Jones.			**VERMONT.**	
	OHIO.		1	Fred'k E. Woodbridge,	7532
1	Benjamin Eggleston,	926	2	Luke P. Poland,	6909
2	Samuel F. Cary, Ind.,	959	3	Worthington C. Smith,	2936
3	Robert C. Schenck,	1067			

a George W. Morgan,† had the original certificate.

Dis.		Maj.	Dis.		Maj.
	SOUTH CAROLINA.			*Tennessee.*	
1	Benjamin F. Whittemore,		8	David A. Nunn,	2868
2	C. C. Bowen,			VIRGINIA.*	
3	Simeon Corley,			WEST VIRGINIA.	
4	James H. Goss,		1	Chester D. Hubbard,	1762
At large,	{ J. M. P. Epping,		2	Bethuel M. Kitchen,	8106
	{ Elias E. Dickson,		3	Daniel Polsley,	1572
	TENNESSEE.			WISCONSIN,	
1	Roderick R. Butler,	10195	1	Halbert E. Paine,	4381
2	Horace Maynard,	8954	2	Benjamin F. Hopkins,	5296
3	William B. Stokes,	6409	3	Amasa Cobb,	5351
4	James Mullens,	6227	4	Charles A. Eldridge,†	2608
5	John Trimble,	6194	5	Philetus Sawyer,	4994
6	Samuel M. Arnell,	5126	6	Cad'lader C. Washburn,	6495
7	Isaac R. Hawkins,	4019			

DELEGATES FROM TERRITORIES.

ARIZONA.			MONTANA.		
Cole Bashford,		491	James M. Cavanaugh,†		1108
COLORADO.			NEW MEXICO.		
George M. Chilcott,		108	Charles P. Clever,†		97
DAKOTA.			UTAH.		
Walter A. Burleigh,		339	William H. Hooper,		
IDAHO.			WASHINGTON.		
Edward D. Holbrook,†		718	Alvan Flanders,		96

The Senate is composed of 52 Republicans and 12 Democrats. There are 10 vacancies.

The House of Representatives will consist of 176 Republicans, and 51 Democrats, when all now elected have taken their seats. There are 18 vacancies, or districts which have not elected.

Joseph S. Smith,† is Representative elect in the Forty-First Congress from Oregon.

At the time of writing (July 20th) the following named members of the present House of Representatives have been nominated for . re-election : Messrs. Axtell † and Johnson,† of California; Logan, Farnsworth, Washburn, Ingersoll, Cook, Cullom, Burr,† Marshall,† and Raum, of Illinois; Kerr,† Holman,† Coburn, Orth, Shanks and Williams, of Indiana; Loughridge, of Iowa; Lynch and Blaine, of Maine; Beaman, of Michigan; Laflin and Ward, of New York; Lawrence, Ashley, Wilson, Morgan,† (whose seat was vacated) Bingham and Garfield of Ohio; Randall,† O'Neill, Myers, Kelley and Covode, of Pennsylvania; Arnell, of Tennessee. The dominant party in their respective districts have nominated others to succeed Messrs. Harding, Bromwell, Ross,† and Baker, of Illinois; Julian, Washburn and Colfax, of Indiana; Wilson, Price, Dodge and Hubbard, of Iowa; Perham, of Maine; Driggs, of Michigan; Windom, of Minnesota; Lincoln, of New York; Clarke, Shellabarger, Eckley and Spalding, of Ohio; Wilson, Finney and Moorhead, of Pennsylvania; Hubbard, Kitchen and Polsley, of West Virginia.

5

HISTORY OF IMPEACHMENT.

March 2nd, 1867, Congress by a vote of thirty-five to eleven in the Senate, and one hundred and thirty-three to thirty-seven in the House—a strict party vote—passed a law over the veto of the President, to regulate the tenure of certain civil offices. The act provided among other things "that every person holding any civil office to which he has been appointed by and with the advice of the Senate, and every person who shall hereafter be appointed to any such office, &c., shall be entitled to hold such office until a successor shall have been appointed by the President, with the advice and consent of the Senate and duly qualified." It specified that members of the Cabinet shall hold their offices respectively for and during the term of the President by whom they may have been appointed, and for one month thereafter, subject to removal by and with the advice and consent of the Senate. The act likewise provided that the President may for misconduct or other cause, temporarily suspend officers during the recess of the Senate, and on the meeting of that body, he must report his reasons for such action, and if the Senate concurs he may remove the officer and appoint a successor, but if the Senate does not concur the officer resumes the duties of his office. The penalty for the violation of the act is a fine not exceeding ten thousand dollars.

President Johnson suspended Edwin M. Stanton, Secretary of War, from office, August 12th, 1867, and Gen. Grant was appointed *ad interim* to perform the duties of the office. January 13th, 1868, the Senate by a vote of thirty-five to six, voted that they do not concur in the suspension of Mr. Stanton, and General Grant retired and Mr. Stanton resumed his former duties. The Senators voted as follows:

YEAS.—Messrs. Anthony, Cameron, Cattell, Chandler, Cole, Conkling, Conness, Corbett, Cragin, Drake, Edmunds, Ferry, Fessenden, Fowler, Frelinghuysen, Harlan, Howard, Howe, Morgan, Morrill of Maine, Morrill of Vermont, Morton, Nye, Patterson of New Hampshire, Pomeroy, Ramsey, Stewart, Sumner, Thayer, Tipton, Trumbull, Wade, Van Winkle, Williams, Wilson.

NAYS.—Messrs. Bayard, Buckalew, Davis, Dixon, Doolittle, Patterson of Tennessee.

Messrs. Henderson and Hendricks paired, Mr. Ross refused to vote, and Messrs. Grimes, Guthrie, Johnson, Norton, Saulsbury, Sherman, Sprague and Willey were absent.

February 21st, President Johnson issued two orders, one for the removal of Mr. Stanton, and the other designating Adj. Gen. Lorenzo Thomas to perform the duties of Secretary of War *ad interim*. Mr. Stanton sent the order received by him to the two Houses of

Congress, then in session, and by advice refused to give up his office. The Senate in Executive Session resolved that "under the Constitution and laws of the United States, the President has no power to remove the Secretary of War and designate any other officer to perform the duties of that office *ad interim*." The Senators voting in the affirmative were

Messrs. Anthony, Cameron, Cattell, Cole, Conkling, Cragin, Drake, Ferry, Harlan, Morrill of Maine, Morrill of Vermont, Morton, Patterson of New Hampshire, Pomeroy, Ramsey, Ross, Sprague, Stewart, Sumner, Thayer, Tipton, Trumbull, Van Winkle, Wade, Willey, Williams, Wilson, Yates.

In the previous December, an attempt had been made to have Mr. Johnson impeached, but only fifty-seven members (all Republicans) had voted for it, while one hundred and eight members (sixty-seven Republicans and forty-one Democrats) voted in the negative. The act of the President in attempting to remove Mr. Stanton and appoint a Secretary *ad interim*, and the votes of the Senate, January 13th and February 21st, revived the subject of impeachment, and on the twenty-fourth of February by a vote of one hundred and twenty-six to forty seven, the House Resolved, That Andrew Johnson, President of the United States, be impeached of high crimes and misdemeanors.

The Representatives voted as follows:

FOR IMPEACHMENT.

Allison, Iowa.	Clarke, Ohio.	Hooper, Mass.
Ames, Mass.	Cobb, Wisconsin.	Hopkins, Wisconsin.
Anderson, Missouri.	Coburn, Indiana.	Hubbard, Iowa.
Arnell, Tennessee.	Colfax, Indiana.	Hubbard, W. Va.
Ashley, Nevada.	Cook, Illinois.	Hulburd, New York.
Ashley, Ohio.	Cornell, N. Y.	Hunter, Indiana.
Bailey, N. Y.	Covode, Penn.	Ingersoll, Illinois.
Baker, Illinois.	Cullom, Illinois.	Jenckes, R. I.
Baldwin, Mass.	Dawes, Mass.	Judd, Illinois.
Banks, Mass.	Dodge, Iowa.	Julian, Indiana.
Beaman, Michigan.	Driggs, Michigan.	Kelley, Penn.
Beatty, Ohio.	Eckley, Ohio.	Kelsey, New York.
Benton, N. H.	Eggleston, Ohio.	Ketcham, New York.
Bingham, Ohio.	Eliot, Massachusetts.	Kitchen, W. Va.
Blaine, Maine.	Farnsworth, Illinois.	Laflin, New York.
Blair, Michigan.	Ferris, New York.	Lawrence, Penn.
Boutwell, Mass.	Ferry, Michigan.	Lawrence, Ohio.
Bromwell, Illinois.	Fields, New York.	Lincoln, New York.
Broomall, Penn.	Gravely, Missouri.	Loan, Missouri.
Buckland, Ohio.	Griswold, N. Y.	Logan, Illinois.
Butler, Mass.	Halsey, New Jersey.	Loughridge, Iowa.
Cake, Pennsylvania.	Harding, Illinois.	Lynch, Maine.
Churchill, N. Y.	Higby, California.	Mallory, Oregon.
Clarke, Kansas.	Hill, New Jersey.	Marvin, New York.

FOR IMPEACHMENT, *(Concluded.)*

McCarthy, New York.
McClurg, Missouri.
Mercur, Penn.
Miller, Penn.
Moore, New Jersey.
Moorhead, Penn.
Morrell, Penn.
Mullins, Tennessee.
Myers, Pennsylvania.
Newcomb, Missouri.
Nunn, Tennessee.
Orth, Indiana.
O'Neill, Pennsylvania.
Paine, Wisconsin.
Perham, Maine.
Peters, Maine.
Pike, Maine.
Pile, Missouri.

Plants, Ohio.
Poland, Vermont.
Polsley, W. Va.
Price, Iowa.
Raum, Illinois.
Robertson, N. Y.
Sawyer, Wisconsin.
Schenck, Ohio.
Scofield, Penn.
Selye, New York.
Shanks, Indiana.
Smith, Vermont.
Spaulding, Ohio.
Starkweather, Conn.
Stevens, N. H.
Stevens, N. H.
Stokes, Tennessee.
Taffe, Nebraska.

Taylor, Penn.
Trowbridge, Mich.
Twichell, Mass.
Upson, Michigan.
Van Aernam, N. Y.
Van Horn, N. Y.
Van Wyck, N. Y.
Ward, New York,
Washburn, Wis.
Washburne, Illinois.
Washburn, Mass.
Welker, Ohio.
Williams, Penn.
Wilson, Iowa.
Wilson, Ohio.
Wilson, Penn.
Windom, Minnesota.
Woodbridge, Vt.

Total, 126—all Republicans.

AGAINST IMPEACHMENT.

Adams, Kentucky.
Archer, Maryland.
Axtell, California.
Barnes, New York.
Barnum, Conn.
Beck, Kentucky.
Boyer, Pennsylvania.
Brooks, New York.
Burr, Illinois.
Cary, Ohio.
Chanler, New York.
Eldridge, Wisconsin.
Fox, New York.
Getz, Pennsylvania.
Glossbrenner, Penn.
Golladay, Kentucky.

Grover, Kentucky.
Haight, New Jersey.
Holman, Indiana.
Hotchkiss, Conn.
Hubbard, Conn.
Humphrey, N. Y.
Johnson, California.
Jones, Kentucky.
Kerr, Indiana.
Knott, Kentucky.
Marshall, Illinois.
McCormick, Mo.
McCullough, Md.
Morgan,* Ohio.
Morrissey, New York.
Mungen, Ohio.

Niblack, Indiana.
Nicholson, Delaware.
Phelps, Maryland.
Pruyn, New York.
Randall, Penn.
Ross, Illinois.
Sitgreaves, N. J.
Stewart, New York.
Stone, Maryland.
Taber, New York.
Trimble, Kentucky.
Van Auken, Penn.
Van Trump, Ohio.
Wood, New York.
Woodward, Penn.

Total, 47—All Democrats except Mr. Cary, who claims to be an Independent Republican, though elected by Democrats.

ABSENT OR NOT VOTING.

Benjamin, Missouri.
Butler, Tennessee.
Dixon, Rhode Island.
Donnelly, Minnesota.
Ela, New Hampshire.
Finney, Penn.

Garfield, Ohio.
Hawkins, Tennessee.
Koontz, Penn.
Maynard, Tennessee.
Pomeroy, New York.
Robinson, New York.

Shellabarger, Ohio.
Thomas, Maryland.
Trimble, Tennessee.
Van Horn, Missouri.
Washburn, Indiana.
Williams, Indiana.

Total, 18—all Republicans except Mr. Robinson.

*Seat since given Columbus Delano, Republican.

The Senate was notified February 25th, and the Articles of Impeachment were presented to that body March 4th. The following were the gist of the articles:

ARTICLE 1 Charged that the President did unlawfully, and in violation of the Constitution and laws of the United States, issue an order in writing, for the removal of Edwin M. Stanton from the office of Secretary of War, the same being done without the advice and consent of the Senate, then being in session.

ART. 2 Charged that the President, in violation of the Constitution of the United States, and contrary to the provisions of the Tenure of Office Act, without the advice and consent of the Senate of the United States, then in session, and without authority of law, did appoint one Lorenzo Thomas to be Secretary of War *ad interim*.

ART. 3 Reiterated the facts with regard to Thomas' appointment, founding the additional charge of illegality upon the fact of no vacancy having happened in said office of Secretary for the Department of War during the recess of the Senate, and no vacancy existing in said office at the time.

ART. 4 Charged that the President conspired with Thomas and others to deprive Secretary Stanton of his office, contrary to the provisions of an act entitled " An Act to define and punish certain conspiracies," approved July 31, 1861.

ART. 5 Charged that the President conspired with Thomas and others to defeat the execution of the Tenure of Office Act.

ART. 6 Charged the President with unlawfully conspiring with Thomas by force to seize, take and possess the property of the United States, in the War Department, contrary to the conspiracy act, and with intent to violate the Tenure of Office Act.

ART. 7 Charged that the President in conspiring to prevent the execution of the Tenure of Office Act, did unlawfully attempt to prevent Secretary Stanton from holding his office, and did commit a high misdemeanor in office.

ART. 8 Charged that the President, with intent unlawfully to control the disbursements of the moneys appropriated for the military service and for the Department of War, did appoint Thomas to be Secretary of War *ad interim*.

ART. 9 Charged the President with endeavoring to induce Gen. Emory to violate the laws and to receive and obey orders from him (the President) contrary to law.

ART. 10 Charged that the President, unmindful of his duties and the dignity of his office, and the harmony which ought to exist between the different branches of the Government, and designing to bring Congress into contempt, did on certain specified days, as well as on other occasions, deliver with a loud voice certain intemperate, inflammatory and scandalous harangues, and did therein utter loud threats and bitter menaces as well against Congress as the laws of the United States duly enacted thereby, amid the cries, jeers and laughter of the multitude then assembled and in hearing — reference being had to speeches at Washington, Cleveland and St. Louis, in 1866.

ART. 11 Charged the President with publicly denying the legality of Congress, or that its legislation was binding upon him; and with attempting to prevent the execution of the Tenure of Office Act; with attempting to prevent Secretary Stanton's resuming his office although the Senate refused to concur in his suspension; and with attempting to defeat the execution of an appropriation act and also the act providing for the government of the rebel States.

The trial commenced March 30th and closed May 6th. It was conducted by Messrs. John A. Bingham, of Ohio, George S. Boutwell, and Benjamin F. Butler, of Massachusetts, John A. Logan, of Illinois, Thaddeus Stevens, and Thomas Williams, of Pennsylvania, and James F. Wilson, of Iowa, as Managers on the part of the House of Representatives. The President was defended by the following named counsel: Benjamin R. Curtis, of Massachusetts, William M. Evarts, of New York, Henry Stanbery and William S. Groesbeck, of Ohio, and Thomas A. R. Nelson, of Tennessee, all eminent lawyers.

After one or two postponements, May 16th was fixed as the time for taking the vote, and the eleventh article was voted upon. The Court then adjourned till Tuesday, May 26th, when the second and third articles were voted on with the same result as before. The Senators voted as follows on each occasion:

GUILTY.

Anthony, R. I.	Frelinghuysen, N. J.	Sherman, Ohio.
Cameron, Pa.	Harlan, Iowa.	Sprague, R. I.
Cattell, N. J.	Howard, Mich.	Stewart, Nevada.
Chandler, Mich.	Howe, Wis.	Sumner, Mass.
Cole, Cal.	Morgan, N. Y.	Thayer, Nebraska.
Conkling, N. Y.	Morrill, Vt.	Tipton, "
Conness, Cal.	Morrill, Me.	Wade, Ohio.
Corbett, Oregon.	Morton, Ind.	Willey, W. Va.
Cragin, N. H.	Nye, Nevada.	Williams, Oregon.
Drake, Mo.	Patterson, N. H.	Wilson, Mass.
Edmunds, Vt.	Pomeroy, Kansas.	Yates, Ill.
Ferry, Ct.	Ramsey, Minn.	

Total, 35.—All Republicans.

NOT GUILTY.

Bayard, Del.	Grimes, Iowa.	Patterson, Tenn.
Buckalew, Pa.	Henderson, Mo.	Ross, Kansas.
Davis, Ky.	Hendricks, Ind.	Saulsbury, Del.
Dixon, Ct.	Johnson, Md.	Trumbull, Ill.
Doolittle, Wis.	McCreery, Ky.	Van Winkle, W. Va.
Fessenden, Me.	Norton, Minn.	Vickers, Md.
Fowler, Tenn.		

Total, 19. Messrs. Fessenden, Fowler, Grimes, Henderson, Ross, Trumbull and Van Winkle are Republicans; the others Democrats.

Less than two-thirds having voted guilty, a verdict of acquittal was entered upon the three articles, and on motion the Court adjourned *sine die*, by a vote of 34 to 16.

NATIONAL REPUBLICAN CONVENTION, 1868.

This body assembled in the Opera House, Chicago, on Wednesday, May 20th, every State and Territory having been represented. Governor Marcus L. Ward, of New Jersey, chairman of the National Republican Committee, called to order. General Carl Schurz, of Missouri, was temporary chairman, and General Joseph R. Hawley, of Connecticut, permanent President, with one Vice President and Secretary for each State. The first day was devoted to preliminary business and listening to speeches. On Thursday, 21st, the following platform was reported and unanimously adopted.

THE NATIONAL REPUBLICAN PARTY OF THE UNITED STATES, assembled in National Convention in the city of Chicago, on the 21st day of May, 1868, make the following Declaration of Principles:

I. We congratulate the country on the assured success of the Reconstruction policy of Congress, as evinced by the adoption, in the majority of the States lately in rebellion, of Constitutions securing Equal, Civil and Political Rights to all, and it is the duty of the Government to sustain these institutions and to prevent the people of such States from being remitted to a state of anarchy.

II. The guaranty by Congress of Equal Suffrage to all loyal men at the South was demanded by every consideration of public safety, of gratitude, and of justice, and must be maintained; while the question of Suffrage in all the loyal States properly belongs to the people of those States.

III. We denounce all forms of Repudiation as a national crime, and the national honor requires the payment of the public indebtedness in the utmost good faith to all creditors at home and abroad, not only according to the letter but the spirit of the laws under which it was contracted.

IV. It is due to the Labor of the Nation that taxation should be equalized, and reduced as rapidly as the national faith will permit.

V. The National Debt, contracted, as it has been, for the preservation of the Union for all time to come, should be extended over a fair period for redemption; and it is the duty of Congress to reduce the rate of interest thereon, whenever it can be honestly done.

VI. That the best policy to diminish our burden of debt is to so improve our credit that capitalists will seek to loan us money at lower rates of interest than we now pay, and must continue to pay so long as repudiation, partial or total, open or covert, is threatened or suspected.

VII. The Government of the United States should be administered with the strictest economy; and the corruptions which have been so shamefully nursed and fostered by Andrew Johnson call loudly for radical reform.

VIII. We profoundly deplore the untimely and tragic death of Abraham Lincoln, and regret the accession to the Presidency of Andrew Johnson, who has acted treacherously to the people who elected him and the cause he was pledged to support; who has usurped high legislative and judicial functions; who has refused to execute the laws; who has used his high office to induce other officers to ignore and violate the laws; who has employed his executive powers to render insecure the property, the peace, liberty and life, of the citizen; who has abused the pardoning power; who has denounced the National Legislature as unconstitutional; who has persistently and corruptly resisted by every means in his power, every proper attempt at the reconstruction of the States lately in rebellion; who has perverted the public patronage into an engine of wholesale corruption; and who has been justly impeached for high crimes and misdemeanors, and properly pronounced guilty thereof by the vote of thirty-five Senators.

IX. The doctrine of Great Britain and other European powers that, because a man is once a subject he is always so, must be resisted at every hazard by the United States, as a relic of feudal times, not authorized by the laws of nations, and at war with our national honor and independence. Naturalized citizens are entitled to protection in all their rights of citizenship, as though they were native-born; and no citizen of the United States, native or naturalized, must be liable to arrest and imprisonment by any foreign power for acts done or words spoken in this country; and if so arrested and imprisoned, it is the duty of the Government to interfere in his behalf.

X. Of all who were faithful in the trials of the late war, there were none entitled to more especial honor than the brave soldiers and seamen who endured the hardships of campaign and cruise, and imperiled their lives in the service of the country; the bounties and pensions provided by the laws for these brave defenders of the nation, are obligations never to be forgotten; the widows and orphans of the gallant dead are the wards of the people—a sacred legacy bequeathed to the nation's protecting care.

XI. Foreign immigration, which in the past has added so much to the wealth, development and resources and increase of power to this republic, the asylum of the oppressed of all nations, should be fostered and encouraged by a liberal and just policy.

XII. This Convention declares itself in sympathy with all oppressed peoples struggling for their rights.

Resolved, That we highly commend the spirit of magnanimity and forbearance with which the men who have served in the Rebellion, but now frankly and honestly co-operate with us in restoring the peace of the country and reconstructing the Southern State Governments upon the basis of impartial justice and equal rights, are received back into the communion of the loyal people; and we favor the removal of the disqualifications and restrictions imposed upon the late Rebels in the same measure as their spirit of loyalty will direct, and so may be consistent with the safety of the loyal people.

Resolved, That we recognize the great principles laid down in the immortal Declaration of Independence as the true foundation of democratic government, and we hail with gladness every effort toward making these principles a living reality on every inch of American soil.

After the adoption of the platform the name of GEN. ULYSSES S. GRANT was proposed as the candidate for President of the United States, and the roll of States was called. Every delegate voted for Gen. Grant, and amid great enthusiasm he was declared unanimously nominated, having received 650 votes.

The Convention next proceeded to ballot for Vice President, a number of names having been presented for that office. The following was the result of the five ballotings which followed:

	1st.	2nd.	3rd.	4th.	5th.
Schuyler Colfax, Ind.	118	149	164	186	224
Benjamin F. Wade, Ohio,	149	170	178	204	199
Reuben E. Fenton, N. Y.,	132	140	130	144	137
Henry Wilson, Mass.,	119	113	101	87	61
Andrew G. Curtin, Pa.,	52	45	30		
Hannibal Hamlin, Me.,	30	30	25	25	19
James Speed, Ky.,	22				
James Harlan, Iowa,	16				
J. A. J. Cresswell, Md.,	14				
Wm. D. Kelley, Pa.,	6				

Before the announcement of the fifth ballot many States transferred their votes to Mr. Colfax and he was declared to have 522; Fenton, 75; Wade, 42; Wilson, 11. Gen. Sickles, of New York, moved to make the nomination of SCHUYLER COLFAX unanimous and the motion was carried. The convention soon after closed its proceedings.

THE REPUBLICAN CANDIDATES.

GEN. ULYSSES S. GRANT, candidate for President, was born in Mount Pleasant, Clermont County, Ohio, April 27th, 1822. He graduated at West Point in 1843, and was brevetted Second Lieutenant. He was assigned to duty as Second Lieutenant of Infantry in 1845, and was in active service during the Mexican war. For gallant services at Molina del Rey he was made First Lieutenant, and again distinguished himself at Chapultepec, for which he was brevetted Captain in 1850. After the

Mexican war, he was assigned to duty on the Pacific coast, and in 1853 he received a full commission as Captain, but resigned the next year, and for several years subsequent he was engaged in private pursuits, first working on a farm near St. Louis, and afterward was interested with his father in the leather business at Galena, Illinois. When the rebellion commenced, in 1861, he at once offered his services to Governor (now Senator) Yates, of Illinois, and in June of that year was commissioned Colonel of the 21st Illinois Regiment, and two months later was promoted as Brigadier General of Volunteers by President Lincoln. He soon after drove the rebels from the vicinity of Paducah, Kentucky, and performed other good work, but his first great victories were the capture of Forts Henry and Donelson, in February, 1862, the terms given in the latter case to Gen. Simon B. Buckner, the rebel commander, being "unconditional surrender." Gen. Grant was immediately promoted to the rank of Major General, and on April 7th and 8th following he fought the battle of Pittsburg Landing, the rebel General A. S. Johnston, having been killed. In July, 1862, Gen. Grant, was made commander of the Department of Tennessee, and soon after occupied Memphis and Holly Springs. After an investment of several months, Vicksburg surrendered to Gen. Grant, July 4th, 1863, with Gen. Pemberton's rebel army, numbering 31,000 men. This with the great Union victory at Gettysburg the day before, caused great rejoicing in the loyal North. Gen. Grant was immediately after the surrender of Vicksburg appointed Major General in the regular army. He remained at the head of the Western Army planning several victories, until March 2d, 1864, when he was appointed Lieutenant General, and immediately thereafter assumed command of all the Union armies, his immediate duties being with the Army of the Potomac. May 3d, the latter Army crossed the Rapidan, and on the 5th, 6th and 7th, the battles of the Wilderness were fought, and on the 11th, Gen. Grant after a summary of the events of the preceding few days, said—"I propose to fight it out on this line if it takes all summer." The siege of Richmond was fairly inaugurated June 14th, and the lines were being constantly contracted from that date until the latter part of March, 1865, when commenced the final battles of the war, which in one week terminated by the capture of Richmond, April 2d, and on the 9th of that month Gen. Robert E. Lee, surrendered the main rebel Army to Gen. Grant. July 25th, 1866, Gen. Grant was appointed General of the Armies of the United, States, the highest military title ever conferred in this country, and which rank he still holds. He served as Secretary of War *ad interim* from August 12th, 1867, to January 13th, 1868, when in obedience to a vote of the United States Senate he retired that Edwin M. Stanton might be restored to the office from which he had been suspended. May 21st, 1868, the Union Republican National Convention unanimously nominated Gen. Grant as candidate for President of the United States.

HON. SCHUYLER COLFAX, candidate for Vice President, is a native of the city of New York, born March 23d, 1823. He received a fair common school education, and in 1836, removed with his mother's family to South Bend, Indiana. He was clerk in a store for a time, but soon after reaching his majority, became proprietor and editor of the *St. Joseph's Register*, published at South Bend. In 1848 and 1852 he was delegate to the Whig National Conventions, serving as a secretary of each. In 1850 he was a member of the Indiana Constitutional Convention, and the following year he was a candidate for Representative in Congress, but was defeated by less than 300 majority. He was successful in 1854 and has been six times re-elected. Soon after he entered Congress he became a prominent member on the Republican side, and for two successive sessions was chairman of the committee on Post Offices and Post Roads. He was elected Speaker of the House of Representatives in 1863, and will have served in that capacity six years when his present term expires. In 1865, he made a tour " Across the Continent " to the Pacific, and has lectured on his tour in the principal cities of the North. May 21st, 1868, he was nominated by the Union Republican National Convention as candidate for Vice President of the United States, over several competitors, and the nomination was afterward made unanimous.

GEN. GRANT'S LETTER OF ACCEPTANCE.

To Gen. JOSEPH R. HAWLEY, President of the National Union Republican Convention: In formally accepting the nomination of the National Union Republican Convention of the 21st of May inst., it seems proper that some statement of views beyond the mere acceptance of the nomination should be expressed. The proceedings of the Convention were marked with wisdom, moderation, and patriotism, and I believe express the feelings of the great mass of those who sustained the country through its recent trials. I endorse the resolutions. If elected to the office of President of the United States, it will be my endeavor to administer all the laws in good faith, with economy, and with the view of giving peace, quiet and protection everywhere. In times like the present it is impossible, or at least eminently improper to lay down a policy to be adhered to, right or wrong, through an administration of four years. New political issues, not foreseen, are constantly arising; the views of the public on old ones are constantly changing, and a purely administrative officer should always be left free to execute the will of the people. I always have respected that will, and always shall. Peace and universal prosperity—its sequence—with economy of administration will lighten the burden of taxation, while it constantly reduces the national debt. Let us have peace.

With great respect, your obedient servant,

U. S. GRANT.

Washington, D. C., May 29, 1868.

MR. COLFAX'S LETTER OF ACCEPTANCE.

Hon. J. R. HAWLEY, &c.,—*Dear Sir:* The platform adopted by the patriotic Convention over which you presided, and the resolutions which so happily supplement it, so entirely agree with my views as to a just national policy that my thanks are due to the Delegates as much for this clear and auspicious declaration of principles as for the nomination with which I have been honored, and which I gratefully accept. When a great Rebellion, which imperiled the national existence, was at last overthrown, the duty of all others, devolving on those entrusted with the responsibilities of legislation, evidently was to require that the revolted States should be re-admitted to participation in the Government against which they had erred only on such a basis as to increase and fortify, not to weaken or endanger, the strength and power of the nation. Certainly no one ought to have claimed that they should be readmitted under such rule that their organization as States could ever again be used, as at the opening of the war, to defy the national authority or to destroy the national unity. This principle has been the pole-star of those who have inflexibly insisted on the Congressional policy, your Convention so cordially indorsed. Baffled by Executive opposition, and by persistent refusals to accept any plan of reconstruction proffered by Congress, justice and public safety at last combined to teach us that only by an enlargement of suffrage in those States could the desired end be attained, and that it was even more safe to give the ballot to those who loved the Union than to those who had sought ineffectually to destroy it. The assured success of this legislation is being written on the adamant of history, and will be our triumphant vindication. More clearly, too, than ever before, does the nation now recognize that the greatest glory of a republic is that it throws the shield of its protection over the humblest and weakest of its people, and vindicates the rights of the poor and the powerless as faithfully as those of the rich and the powerful. I rejoice, too, in this connection, to find in your platform the frank and fearless avowal that naturalized citizens must be protected abroad at every hazard, as though they were native-born. Our whole people are foreigners, or descendants of foreigners; our fathers established by arms their right to be called a nation. It remains for us to establish the right to welcome to our shores all who are willing, by oaths of allegiance, to become American citizens. Perpetual allegiance, as claimed abroad, is only another name for perpetual bondage, and would make all slaves to the soil where first they saw the light. Our National cemeteries prove how faithfully these oath of fidelity to their adopted land have been sealed in the life blood of thousands upon thousands. Should we not, then, be faithless to the dead if we did not protect their living brethren in the full enjoyment of that nationality for which, side by side, with the native born, our soldiers of foreign birth laid down their lives. It was fitting too, that the representatives of a party which had proved so true to national duty in time of war, should speak so clearly in time of peace for the maintenance untarnished of the national honor, national credit and good faith as regards its debt, the cost of our national existence. I do not need to extend this reply by further comment on a platform which has elicited such hearty approval throughout the land. The debt of gratitude it acknowledges to the brave men who saved the Union from destruction, the frank approval of amnesty based on repentance and loyalty, the demand for the most thorough economy and honesty in the Government, the sympathy of the party of liberty whith all throughout the world who longed for the liberty we here enjoy, and the recognition of the sublime principles of the Declaration of Independence, are worthy of the organization, on whose banners they are to be written in the coming contest. Its past record cannot be blotted out or forgotten. If there had been no Republican party, Slavery would to-day cast its baleful shadow over the republic. If there had been no Republican party, a free press, and free speech would be as unknown from the Potomac to the Rio Grande as ten years ago. If the Republican party could have been stricken from existence when the banner of Rebellion was unfurled, and when the response of "No Coercion" was heard at the North, we would have had no nation to-day. But for the Republican party daring to risk the odium of tax, and draft laws, our flag could not have been kept flying in the field until the long hoped for victory came. Without a Republican party the Civil Rights bill—the guarantee of equality under the law to the humble, and the defenceless, as well as to the strong—would not be to-day upon our National Statute book. With such inspiration from the past, and following the example of the founders of the Republic, who called the victorious General of the Revolution to preside over the land his triumphs had saved from its enemies, I cannot doubt that our labors will be crowned with success; and it will be a success that shall bring restored hope, confidence, prosperity, and progress South as well as North, West as well as East, and above all, the blessings under Providence of National concord and peace.

Very truly yours,
SCHUYLER COLFAX.

A SOLDIERS' AND SAILORS' CONVENTION was held at Chicago, May 19th, 1868. Gen. Lucius Fairchild, of Wisconsin, presided. The resolutions endorsed Gen. Grant for President, pledged their earnest and active support to the Republican party, approved of the impeachment of Andrew Johnson, demand protection for naturalized citizens abroad, and tender sympathy and support to the loyal men of the South.

THE mystic cords of memory, stretching from every battle-field and patriot grave to every living heart and hearth-stone all over this broad land, will yet swell the chorus of the Union, when again touched, as surely they will be, by the better angels of our nature.—ABRAHAM LINCOLN'S *first inaugural address.*

WITH malice toward none, with charity for all, with firmness in the right, as God gives us to see the right, let us strive on to finish the work we are in, to bind up the nation's wounds, to care for him who shall have borne the battle and for his widow and orphans, to do all which may achieve and cherish a just and lasting peace among ourselves and with all nations.—ABRAHAM LINCOLN'S *last inaugural address.*

DEMOCRATIC NATIONAL CONVENTION, 1868.

This body met in Tammany Hall, New York, Saturday, July 4th, and was called to order by August Belmont, of New York, chairman of the Democratic National Committee. Henry L. Palmer, of Wisconsin, was chosen temporary President. The first day was occupied with the transaction of preliminary business common to such assemblies.

On Monday, 6th, Hon. Horatio Seymour, of New York, was elected permanent President, and a Vice President and Secretary were reported and elected for each State. Little progress was made on this day, and the convention adjourned until Tuesday, 7th, when the committee on resolutions made their report, and after discussion it was unanimously adopted as

THE DEMOCRATIC PLATFORM.

THE DEMOCRATIC PARTY in National Convention assembled, reposing its trust in the intelligence, patriotism, and discriminating justice of the people, standing upon the Constitution as the foundation and limitation of the powers of the Government, and the guaranty of the liberties of the citizen, and recognizing the questions of Slavery and Secession as having been settled for all time to come by the war, or the voluntary action of the Southern States in constitutional conventions assembled, and never to be renewed or re-agitated, do with the return of peace demand:

I. Immediate restoration of all the States to their rights in the Union, under the Constitution, and of civil government to the American people.

II. Amnesty for all past political offences and the regulation of the elective franchise in the States by their citizens.

III. Payment of the public debt of the United States as rapidly as practicable, all moneys drawn from the people by taxation, except so much as is requisite for the necessities of the Government economically administered, being honestly applied to such payment, and, where the obligations of the Government do not expressly state upon their face, or the law under which they were issued does not provide that they shall be paid in coin, they ought, in right and in justice, be paid in the lawful money of the United States.

IV. Equal taxation of every species of property, according to its real value, including Government bonds and other public securities.

V. One currency for the Government and the people, the laborer and the office-holder, the pensioner and the soldier, the producer and the bondholder.

VI. Economy in the administration of the Government, the reduction of the standing army and navy, the abolition of the Freedmen's Bureau and all political instrumentalities designed to secure negro supremacy; simplification of the system and discontinuance of inquisitorial modes of assessing and collecting Internal Revenue, so that the burden of taxation may be equalized and lessened, the credit of the Government increased, and the currency made good, the repeal of all enactments for enrolling the State Militia into National forces in time of peace, and a tariff for revenue upon foreign imports, and such equal taxation under the Internal Revenue laws as will afford incidental protection to domestic manufactures, and as will, without impairing the revenue, impose the least burden upon and best promote and encourage the great industrial interests of the country.

VII. Reform of abuses in the Administration, the expulsion of corrupt men from office, the abrogation of useless offices, the restoration of rightful authority to and the independence of the Executive and Judicial Departments of the Government, and the subordination of the military to the civil power, to the end that the usurpations of Congress and the despotism of the sword may cease.

VIII. Equal rights and protection for naturalized and native born citizens at home and abroad, the assertion of American nationality which shall command the respect of foreign powers and furnish an example and encouragement to people struggling for national integrity, constitutional liberty, and individual rights; and the maintenance of the rights of naturalized citizens, against the absolute doctrine of immutable allegiance and the claims of foreign powers to punish them for alleged crime committed beyond their jurisdiction.

In demanding these measures and reforms we arraign the Radical party for its disregard of right and the unparalleled oppression and tyranny which have marked its career. After the most solemn and unanimous pledge of both Houses of Congress to prosecute the war exclusively for the maintenance of the Government and the preservation of the Union under the Constitution, it has repeatedly violated that most sacred pledge under which alone was rallied that noble volunteer army which carried our flag to victory. Instead of restoring the Union, it has, so far as in its power, dissolved it, and subjected ten States in time of profound peace to military despotism and negro supremacy. It has nullified there the right of trial by jury; it has abolished the habeas corpus, that most sacred writ of liberty; it has overthrown the freedom of speech and the press; it has substituted arbitrary seizures and arrests, and military trials, and secret star-chamber inquisitions for the constitutional tribunals; it has disregarded in time of peace the right of the people to be free from searches and seizures, it has entered the post and telegraph offices, and even the private rooms of individuals, and seized their private papers and letters without any specific charge or notice of affidavit, as required by the organic law; it has converted the American capitol into a Bastile; it has established a system of spies and of espionage to which no constitutional monarchy of Europe would dare to resort; it has abolished the right of appeal on important constitutional questions to the supreme judicial tribunals, and threatens to curtail or destroy its original jurisdiction which is irrevocably vested by the Constitution; while the learned Chief-Justice has been subjected to the most atrocious calumnies merely because he would not prostitute his high office to the support of the false and partisan charges preferred against the President. Its corruption and extravagance have exceeded anything known in history; and by its frauds and monopolies it has nearly doubled the burden of the debt created by the war. It has stripped the President of his Constitutional power of appointment, even of his own Cabinet. Under its repeated assaults the pillars of the Government are rocking on their base, and should it succeed in November next and inaugurate its President, we will meet as a subject and conquered people amid the ruins of liberty and the shattered fragments of the Constitution; and we do declare and resolve, that ever since the people of the United States threw off all subjection to the British Crown the privilege and trust of suffrage have belonged to the several States, and have been granted, regulated and controlled exclusively by the political power of each State respectively, and that any attempt by Congress, on any pretext whatever, to deprive any State of this right, or interfere with its exercise, is a flagrant usurpation of power which can find no warrant in the Constitution; and, if sanctioned by the people, will subvert our form of government, and can only end in a single centralized and consolidated government, in which the separate existence of the States will be entirely absorbed, and an unqualified despotism be established in place of a Federal Union of coequal States; and that we regard the reconstruction acts (so called) of Congress, as such a usurpation and unconstitutional, revolutionary and void; that our soldiers and sailors who carried the flag of our country to victory against a most gallant and determined foe, must ever be gratefully remembered and all the guarantees given in their favor must be faithfully carried into execution. That the public lands should be distributed as widely as possible among the people, and should be disposed of either under the pre-emption or homestead laws, and sold in reasonable quantities, and to none but actual occupants, at the minimum price established by the Government. When grants of the public lands may be allowed necessary for the encouragement of important public improvements, the proceeds of the sale of such lands, and not the lands themselves, should be so applied.

That the President of the United States, Andrew Johnson, in exercising the power of his high office in resisting the aggressions of Congress upon the Constitutional rights of the States and the people, is entitled to the gratitude of the whole American people, and in behalf of the Democratic party we tender him our thanks for his patriotic efforts in that regard. Upon this platform the Democratic party appeal to every patriot, including all the Conservative element, and all who desire to support the Constitution and restore the Union, forgetting all past differences of opinion to unite with us in the present great struggle for the liberties of the people; and that to all such, to whatever party they may have heretofore belonged, we extend the right hand of fellowship, and hail all such co-operating with us as friends and brethren.

6

Preceding the balloting for a candidate for President, the convention reaffirmed the old rule of Democratic National Conventions, requiring two-thirds of all the delegates to nominate. As there were 317 delegates in attendance from thirty-seven States, 212 were therefore required to nominate. Nominations of candidates for President were called for, and the names of James E. English of Connecticut, George H. Pendleton of Ohio, Winfield S. Hancock of Pennsylvania, Asa Packer of Pennsylvania, Sanford E. Church of New York, Joel Parker of New Jersey, Andrew Johnson of Tennessee, and James R. Doolittle of Wisconsin, were severally proposed, to which was afterward added those of Thos. A. Hendricks of Indiana, Frank P. Blair, of Missouri, and others. On Tuesday six ballotings were taken, on Wednesday twelve, and on Thursday four, making in all twenty-two. The results of the several ballotings were as follows:

Ballotings.	1	2	3	4	5	6	7	8	9
G. H. Pendleton,	105	104	119½	118½	122	122½	137½	156½	144
A. Johnson,	65	52	34½	32	24	21	12½	6	5½
S. E. Church,	34	33	33	33	33	33	33		
W. S. Hancock,	33½	40½	45½	43½	46	47	42½	28	34½
Asa Packer,	26	26	26	26	27	27	26	26	26½
J. E. English,	16	12½	7½	7½	7	6	6	6	6
J. R. Doolittle,	13	12½	12	12	15	12	17	12	12
Joel Parker,	13	15½	13	13	13	13	7	7	7
R. Johnson,	8½	8	11	8					
T. A. Hendricks,	2½	2	9½	11½	19½	30	34½	75	80½
F. P. Blair,	½	10½	4½	2	9½	5	½	½	½
T. Ewing, Jr.,		½	1	1					
H. Seymour,				9					
J. Q. Adams,					1				

Ballotings,	10	11	12	13	14	15	16	17	18
G. H. Pendleton,	147½	144½	145½	134½	130	129½	107½	70½	56½
T. A. Hendricks,	82½	88	89	81	84½	82½	70½	80	87
W. S. Hancock,	34	32½	30	48½	56	79½	113½	137½	144½
Asa Packer,	27½	26	26	26	26				
J. R. Doolittle,	12	12½	12½	13	13	12	12	12	12
Joel Parker,	7	7	7	7	7	7	7	7	3½
A. Johnson,	6	5½	4½	4½		5½	5½	6	10
F. P. Blair,	½	½	½	½					
G. B. McClellan,			1						
S. P. Chase,			1	½				½	½
Franklin Pierce,				1					
J. T. Hoffman,								3	3

Mr. Pendleton was withdrawn after the 18th balloting.

Ballotings.	19	20	21	22
W. S. Hancock,	136½	142½	139½	
T. A. Hendricks,	107½	121	132	
Asa Packer,	22			
F. P. Blair,	13½	13		
S. J. Field,	13	9	8	
J. R. Doolittle,	12	12	12	
J. E. English,	6	16	19	··
T. H. Seymour,	6	2		
S. P. Chase,	½		4	
A. Johnson,		5		
G. B. McClellan,				½
HORATIO SEYMOUR,				317

As the twenty-second balloting was progressing, Gen. McCook, of Ohio, proposed the name of Horatio Seymour in behalf of his delegation, saying that the latter could now accept the nomination without dishonor though it might be against his inclination. Mr. Seymour, who occupied the chair, protested against the use of his name, thanked the convention and the Ohio delegation for the intended honor, but said that he could not receive the nomination without placing himself and the great Democratic party in a false position. He hoped that God would bless them, but their candidate he could not be. Mr. Seymour shortly after called Gen. Price, of Missouri, one of the Vice Presidents, to the chair, and retired from the hall. Several delegates appealed to the convention, and the result was that State after State changed their votes from others to Hon. HORATIO SEYMOUR, and amidst a scene of wild excitement he was declared the unanimous nominee for President.

After a recess, the convention reassembled, and several names were proposed for Vice President, but all were withdrawn in favor of Gen. FRANCIS P. BLAIR, of Missouri, who was unanimously declared the nominee by acclamation. The convention soon after adjourned.

THE DEMOCRATIC CANDIDATES.

HON. HORATIO SEYMOUR, candidate for President, was born in Pompey, Onondaga County, New York, in 1811. He was liberally educated, adopted the profession of law, and commenced its practice in Utica, but inheriting a large property, devoted himself to its care, and abandoned his profession. He first entered public life in 1842 as Mayor of Utica, and member of the Assembly of New York, which latter position he held three or four years, and served as Speaker in 1845. He has always been a Democrat. In 1850 he was the Democratic candidate for Governor and was supported for the same office four times thereafter, having been twice elected, (1852 and 1862) and three times defeated. The votes cast for and against him on each occasion were as follows :

1850	Horatio Seymour,	214,352	Wash. Hunt, Whig,		214,614
1852	" "	264,121	" "		239,736
			Tompkins, F. S.		19,290
1854	" "	156,495	Myron H. Clark, Whig,		156,804
	G. C. Bronson, Dem.	33,890	D. Ullman, K. N.,		122,282
1862	Horatio Seymour,	306,649	J. S. Wadsworth, Rep.,		295,897
1864	" "	361,264	R. E. Fenton, Rep.,		369,557

Mr. Seymour was defeated the first time by 262 majority, elected the second time by 24,385 ; next defeated by 309 ; then elected by 10,752, and defeated the third time by 8,293 votes. Gov. Seymour's last term was during the late rebellion, and he opposed the policy of the administration of President Lincoln, though as Governor of the State of New York, he sent forward soldiers. He opposed the draft in 1863, and has been severely censured for his course during the celebrated draft riots in New York City, in July, 1863, it having been charged that while he did not directly encourage the riot, his language in an address made to the rioters was construed as palliating their offence. Mr. Seymour is said not to entertain the views of many members of his party on financial matters, though he also opposes the financial policy of Congress. He presided over the Democratic National Convention held at Chicago in 1864 and at New York the present year. He is an able man, and his name has been mentioned heretofore in connection with the office for which he is now the candidate of a large party. It was generally understood before the recent convention assembled that he was not an aspirant at this time, but the division as to a candidate led to bringing him forward at a moment when it seemed that no other man could secure the nomination.

GEN. FRANCIS P. BLAIR, the candidate for Vice President, is a native of Lexington, Kentucky, born February 19th, 1821. He graduated at Princeton College, studied law, and practiced at St. Louis, Missouri, for many years. He served in the Mexican war as a private under Gen. Doniphan. In 1848, he first became known in political circles as a member of the Free-soil party, was editor of the *Missouri Democrat*, at one time, and in 1852 and 1854 was elected to the Missouri Legislature as an Emancipationist or supporter of Thomas H. Benton. In 1856 he was elected a Republican member of the National House of Representatives, was defeated in 1858, but re-elected in 1860 and 1862, though his election was contested the last time on the ground of fraudulent voting, and the seat given to Mr. Knox, a Radical. He early entered the military service of the Government after the rebellion commenced, as a Colonel of Missouri volunteers, and was soon after promoted to the rank of Brigadier and Major General. He served under Gen. Fremont in Missouri, and was with Gen. Sherman in his march through Georgia and the Carolinas, and performed brave duty. He has for the past few years acted with the Democrats, and was supported by them as a candidate for the Missouri Legislature in 1866, but was not elected. He is a man of considerable ability; and has recently subjected himself to sharp criticism by writing a letter favoring the nullification of the reconstruction acts of Congress by a Democratic President, should one be elected at the next election.

———

MR. SEYMOUR'S SPEECH OF ACCEPTANCE.

[The compiler desired to insert here the letter of Hon. Horatio Seymour, accepting the nomination for the Presidency, but at the time this portion of the Manual went to press, it had not been published; in place of the letter, therefore, is here presented his speech of acceptance, made at a Democratic meeting, held in

Tammany Hall, Friday evening, July 10th, the evening of the next day after his nomination.]

Mr. Chairman and Gentlemen of the Committee—I thank you for the courteous terms in which you have communicated to me the action of the Democratic National Convention. I have no words adequate to express my gratitude for the good will and kindness which that body has shown to me. Its nomination was unsought and unexpected. It was my ambition to take an active part, from which I am now excluded, in the great struggle going on for the restoration of good government, of peace and prosperity to our country. But I have been caught up by the whelming tide that is bearing us on to a great political change, and I find myself unable to resist its pressure. You have also given to me a copy of the resolutions put forth by the Convention, showing its position upon all the great questions which now agitate the country. As the presiding officer of that Convention, I am familiar with their scope and import, and as one of its members I am a party to their terms; they are in accord with my views, and I stand upon them in the contest upon which we are now entering; and I shall strive to carry them out in future wherever I may be placed in public or private life. I congratulate you and all conservative men who seek to restore order, peace, prosperity and good government to our land, upon the evidences everywhere shown that we are to triumph at the next election. Those who are politically opposed to us flattered themselves there would be discord in our councils; they mistook the uncertainties of our views as to the best methods of carrying out our purposes for difference of opinion in regard to those purposes. They mistook an intense anxiety to do no act which should not be wise and judicious for a spirit of discord; but during the lengthened proceedings and earnest discussions of the Convention there has prevailed an entire harmony of intercourse, a patient forbearance and a self-sacrificing spirit which are the sure tokens of a coming victory. Accept for yourselves, gentlemen, my wishes for your future welfare and happiness. In a few days I will answer the communication you have just handed me by letter, as is the customary form.

GEN. BLAIR'S LETTER OF ACCEPTANCE.

Gen. GEORGE W. MORGAN, &c.,—*General:* I take the earliest opportunity of replying to your letter notifying me of my nomination for Vice President of the United States by the National Democratic Convention, held in New York. I accept without hesitation the nomination tendered in a manner so gratifying, and give you and the committee thanks for the kind and complimentary language in which you have conveyed to me the decision of the Convention.

I have carefully read the resolutions adopted by the Convention, and most cordially concur in every principle and sentiment they announce. My opinion upon all the questions which discriminate the great contending parties, have been freely expressed on all suitable occasions, and I do not deem it necessary at this time to reiterate them. The issues upon which the contest turns are clear, and cannot be obscured or distorted by the sophistries of our adversaries. They all resolve themselves into the old and ever recurring struggle of a few men to absorb the political power of the nation. The effort under every conceivable name and disguise, has always characterized the opponents of the Democratic party, but at no time has the attempt assumed a shape so open and daring as in this contest.

The adversaries of free and constitutional government in defiance of the express language of the Constitution, have erected a military despotism in ten of the States of the Union, have taken from the President the power vested in him by the supreme law, and have deprived the Supreme Court of its jurisdiction; the right of trial by jury, and the great writ of right, the habeas corpus, shields of safety for every citizen, and which have descended to us from the earliest traditions of our ancestors and which our revolutionary fathers sought to secure to their posterity forever in the fundamental charter of our liberties, have been ruthlessly trampled under foot by the fragment of a Congress. Whole States and communities of people of our race have been attainted, convicted, condemned and deprived of their rights as citizens without presentment, or trial, or witnesses, but by Congressional enactment of *ex post facto* laws and in defiance of the constitutional prohibition, denying even to a full and legal Congress the authority to pass any bill of attainder or *ex post facto* law. The same usurping authority has substituted as electors in place of the men of our race thus illegally attainted and disfranchised, a host of ignorant negroes, who are supported in idleness with the public money, and combined together to strip the white race of their birthright, through the management of freedmen's bureaus, and the emissaries of conspirators in other States; and to complete the oppression, the military power of the nation has been placed at their disposal, in order to make this barbarism supreme. The military leader under whose prestige this usurping Congress has taken refuge since the condemnation of their schemes by the free people of the North in the elections of the last year, and whom they have selected as their candidate, to shield themselves from the result of their own wickedness and crime, has announced his acceptance of the nomination, and his willingness to maintain their usurpations over eight millions of white people at the South, fixed to the earth with his bayonets. He exclaims, " Let us have peace." " Peace reigns in Warsaw," was the announcement which heralded the doom of the liberties of a nation. "The empire is peace," exclaimed Bonaparte when freedom and its defenders expired under the sharp edge of his sword.

The peace to which Grant invites us is the peace of despotism and death. Those who seek to restore the Constitution by executing the will of the people condemning the reconstruction acts, already pronounced in the elections of last year, (and which will, I am convinced, be still more emphatically expressed by the election of the Democratic candidate as President of the United States,) are denounced as revolutionists by the partizans of this vindictive Congress. Negro suffrage which the popular vote of New York, New Jersey, Pennsylvania, Ohio, Michigan, Connecticut and other States have condemned as expressly against the letter of the Constitution, must stand because their Senators and Representatives have willed it.

If the people shall again condemn these atrocious measures by the election of the Democratic candidate for President, they must not be disturbed. Although decided to be unconstitutional by the Supreme Court, and although the President is sworn to maintain and support the Constitution, the will of a fraction of a Congress, reinforced with its partisan emissaries sent to the South, and supported there by the soldiery, must stand against the will of the people, and the decision of the Supreme Court, and the solemn oath of the President to maintain the Constitution. It is revolutionary to execute the will of the people. It is revolutionary to execute the judgment of the Supreme Court. It is revolutionary in the President to keep inviolate his oath to sustain the Constitution. This false construction of the vital principle of our government is the last resort of those who would have their arbitrary reconstruction sway, and supersede our time honored customs. The nation will say the Constitution must be restored and the will of the people again prevail. The appeal to the peaceful ballot to attain this end is not war—is not revolution. They make war and revolution who attempt to arrest this quiet mode of putting aside military despotism, and the usurpations of a fragment of a Congress asserting absolute power over that benign system of regulated liberty left us by our fathers. This must be allowed to take its course. This is the only road to peace. It will come with the election of the Democratic candidate, and not with the election of that mailed warrior, whose bayonets are now at the throats of eight millions of people in the South, to compel them to support him as a candidate for the Presidency, and to submit to the domination of an alien race of semi-barbarous men. No perversion of truth or audacity of misrepresentation can exceed that which hails this candidate in arms as an angel of peace.

    I am very respectfully,
        Your most obedient servant,   F. P. BLAIR.

FOURTEENTH ARTICLE OF AMENDMENT.

The following is the Fourteenth Article of Amendment to the Constitution of the United States, which the Southern States were required to adopt previous to re-admission, and which is now adopted by the requisite number of three-quarters of all the States :

SECTION 1. All persons born or naturalized in the United States, and subject to the jurisdiction thereof, are citizens of the United States and of the State wherein they reside. No State shall make or enforce any law which shall abridge the privileges or immunities of citizens of the United States; nor shall any State deprive any person of life, liberty, or property, without due process of law, nor deny to any person within its jurisdiction the equal protection of the laws.

SEC. 2. Representatives shall be apportioned among the several States according to their respective numbers, counting the whole number of persons in each State, excluding Indians not taxed. But when the right to vote at any election for the choice of electors for President and Vice President of the United States, Representatives in Congress, the executive and judicial officers of a State, or the members of the Legislature thereof, is denied to any of the male inhabitants of such State, being twenty-one years of age and citizens of the United States, or in any way abridged, except for participation in rebellion or other crime, the basis of representation therein shall be reduced in the proportion which the number of such male citizens shall bear to the whole number of male citizens twenty-one years of age in such State.

SEC. 3. No person shall be a Senator or Representative in Congress, or elector of President and Vice President, or hold any office, civil or military, under the United States, or under any State, who, having previously taken an oath, as a member of Congress, or as an officer of the United States, or as a member of any State Legislature, or as an executive or judicial officer of any State, to support the Constitution of the United States, shall have engaged in insurrection or rebellion against the same, or given aid or comfort to the enemies thereof. But Congress may, by vote of two-thirds of each House, remove such disability.

SEC. 4. The validity of the public debt of the United States authorized by law, including debts incurred for the payment of pensions and bounties for services in suppressing insurrection or rebellion, shall not be questioned. But neither the United States nor any State shall assume or pay any debt or obligation incurred in aid of insurrection or rebellion against the United States, or any claim for the loss or emancipation of any slave: but all such debts, obligations, and claims shall be held illegal and void.

SEC. 5. The Congress shall have power to enforce, by appropriate legislation, the provision of this article.

THE PRESIDENTIAL ELECTION.

The following is a summary of the laws and constitutional requirements in the election of a President and Vice President:

Electors elected on the first Tuesday after the first Monday in November.

The Governor gives notice to electors of their election, before the first Wednesday in December.

Electors meet on the first Wednesday in December, and cast their votes. They then sign three certificates—send a messenger with one to the President of the Senate, at Washington, before the first Wednesday in January—another by mail to the same person, and the third deliver to the United States District Judge, where electors meet.

Each State provides by law for filling any vacancy in the Board of Electors, occasioned by absence, death, or resignation. Such of the electors as are present are generally authorized to fill any vacancy.

On the second Wednesday in February, Congress shall be in session, and open the returns. The President of the Senate shall, in the presence of the House of Representatives, open the certificate of returns, and count the votes. The person having the greatest number of votes for President, if such number be a majority of the whole number of electors, shall be the President.

If no person has a majority as above, the choice is to be made from the highest returned. The members of the House, by States, form themselves into Electoral Committees, and the majority determine which is to be the choice of the State—each State having only one vote.

If neither of the candidates get a majority of the States before the 4th of March, then the Vice President shall act as President.

If no candidate for Vice President has a majority of the electors, then from the two highest candidates the Senate elects the Vice President, each Senator having one vote.

AYER'S HAIR VIGOR.

Yielding to frequent and urgent solicita-tions from persons in all parts of the country who had experienced the virtues of our med-icines, we began, several years ago, a series of investigations which should lead to the production of a really efficient Hair Restorer. After the most exhaustive researches into the diseases of the hair and scalp, and their rem-edies, aided by eminent chemists and physi-ologists, we have the pleasure to offer the public a preparation which cannot fail to win their confidence. It combines the most desirable qualities of the best preparations extant, without their objectionable ones,—the result of a determination to supply what should be both effectual and harmless, whereas, many of the Hair Restorers in the market are feared as dangerous. The large number who have tried the Vigor speak of it in unqualified terms of praise, expressing the fullest satisfaction with its results.

It is a Delightful Dressing,

Rendering the hair soft, pliant and glossy, and perfuming it with a new odor of rare delicacy, much admired by all who have used it. On account of these peculiarities, it is already sought by ladies whose hair is so abundant as to require only a rich dressing. It excites the scalp to excrete its moisture, so that after the Vigor has dissipated, the hair is kept soft by this, its own proper unguent.

Such a HAIR DRESSING as we now supply has been long de-sired,—one which could be relied on to effect known results, with-out being offensive, or injurious to the hair or the general health. Where a preparation is not needed to reproduce nor to color the hair, the use of the Vigor will be found highly beneficial, as tend-ing to keep up the vitality of the growth; and, as a dressing, is superior to any in the market, and is surely the best we can pro-duce. To many the preservation of this great natural ornament is so much an object, that we know we are meeting an urgent want when we supply a safe and agreeable dressing, which beautifies the hair if it is abundant, preserves it if decaying, and restores it and its beauty when they have been lost.

Prepared by DR. J. C. AYER & CO., LOWELL, MASS., and sold by ALL DRUGGISTS EVERYWHERE.

PRICE, TWENTY-FIVE CENTS.

A

POLITICAL MANUAL

FOR THE

CAMPAIGN OF 1868,

FOR USE IN THE

NEW ENGLAND STATES,

CONTAINING THE POPULATION AND LATEST ELECTION
RETURNS OF EVERY TOWN IN NEW ENGLAND,
AND OF EVERY STATE IN THE UNION,
PARTY PLATFORMS, AND OTHER
VALUABLE INFORMATION.

By S. A. McPhetres.

BOSTON:

A. WILLIAMS AND COMPANY,

100 WASHINGTON STREET.

1868.

Press of Stone & Huse, ... Lowell, Mass.

HEADQUARTERS

E. PLURIBUS UNUM.

For every description of Goods for the

POLITICAL CAMPAIGN!

CUTTER, HYDE & CO.,

32 & 36 FEDERAL, and

107, 111 & 113 CONGRESS STREETS,

BOSTON.

CHINESE LANTERNS, in great variety;
CANDLES and HOLDERS, for illumination;
FLAGS, all sizes.

Badges in every Material and Style.

New Styles received every week.

LANTERNS FOR PROCESSIONS,
TORCHES.

And every style and kind of Goods used in a political campaign.

ALL ORDERS ADDRESSED TO

CUTTER, HYDE & CO.,

Importers of Fancy Goods, Toys and Staple Articles.

Agents wanted in every City and Town in New England, to whom a liberal commission will be paid.